The Cloud Chaser

Peter W. Riffle

Michele,
Hope you enjoy The Cloud Chaser!

Printed in 2006 by

Ensinger Printing Service
50 W. Main Street
Adamstown, Pennsylvania 19501

Certificate of Registration Number TXu1-256-887

ISBN 0-9778665-0-5

Manufactured in the United States of America.

Distributed by Pauper Boy Enterprises
Box 616
Adamstown, Pennsylvania 19501
www.thecloudchaser.net

In Memory of Mindy Anne Pinder

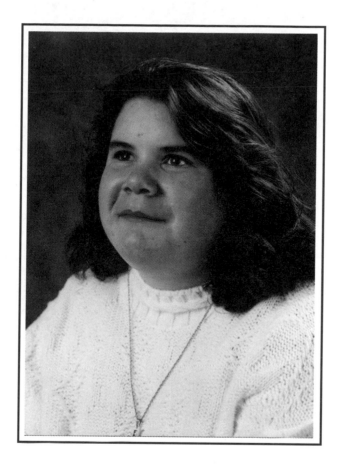

On Monday, September 4, 2000, God put his loving arms around Mindy and called her home. She had fought a long and gallant battle against Batten Disease, an incurable illness that may have destroyed her body, but never her spirit.

Many people are fortunate enough to live longer lives, yet never touch the number of hearts that Mindy touched during her twenty-one short years. I will never forget her sweet personality full of engaging smiles and contagious giggles that were ever present even in the midst of all her trials and tribulations. Mindy made an incredible impact on my life, and I will always treasure the privilege of having known her. With much love, I dedicate *The Cloud Chaser* to her memory.

A Tribute to My Mother

The Cloud Chaser could not go to print without a tribute to my mother – Helen Teel Riffle. No words ever written could adequately express my love and admiration for this wonderful lady. She is the epitome of what every mother should be. I will be forever grateful for the love, guidance, and support she has given to my brother Paul and me. Mother, you are my Cloud Chaser!

How I often saw my mother
as she corrected English papers.

Acknowledgements

The following people have been teachers, college professors, administrators, and coworkers who have influenced my life as not only a teacher but also for molding the person I have become. Words cannot express the appreciation for what they have done for me.

Dr. Gerald Achenbach	Dr. C. Jay Hertzog
Dr. Dion Betts	Mr. Steven Leever
Dr. Constance P. Dent	Mrs. Lisa Magee
Dr. Carl Derr	Dr. Aaron Miller
Dr. Stanley Dubelle	Dr. John Reitz
Mr. Wayne Foley	Mr. Randy Roy
Dr. Lee T. Fredericks	Mr. Herbert Schoenly
Dr. Charles Goodling	Dr. Gerald Slemmer
Mr. Paul Grebinger	Dr. Dale Smith
Mr. John Gurski	Mrs. Cheryl Yocum

Cover art for *The Cloud Chaser* was designed by Harry Gallardo.

I will be forever grateful to my editors, Elaine Schwenk, Helen T. Riffle, and Daniel R. Leininger who took on the task of guiding a fledgling author with a learning disability through the peaks and valleys of writing *The Cloud Chaser*.

Last, but far from least, are the employees and students of the Wilson School District in West Lawn, Pennsylvania, who have made my teaching career so fulfilling.

TABLE OF CONTENTS

FOREWORD

"Teach with your heart; your subject matter will take care of itself," says Peter W. Riffle. Could it be any clearer? Could it be any simpler… yet, could it be any more challenging?

Before reading any further, allow me to provide you with a recommendation. If you are reading this book to discover the latest data regarding educational research analyzed by statistical gurus, stop now. If you are reading this book to hear age-old philosophies of education debated by renowned academicians, stop now. If you are reading this book to learn how to survive in the classroom and become someone that others will refer to as a "darn good teacher," then you've chosen the right book.

The Cloud Chaser brings together stories of real students and their challenges and accomplishments, teaching tips that have been tested and perfected, and Riffle's self-reflections on his personal learning disabilities and how he has overcome those obstacles.

After more than thirty-seven years of teaching, Riffle admits that he knows of no college course that will actually prepare someone for his or her first teaching assignment. He hopes that by sharing his life in the classroom, future teachers and those new to the field, will be better prepared to face the reality of teaching. Through colorful stories about a wide range of students and descriptions of hands-on, trial-and-error classroom strategies, you'll learn how Riffle developed his classroom rules and how he learned to live by them.

You'll find that success grows from risk taking. In one of his examples, Riffle shares a story from many years ago about trust. He tells about when he tacked a twenty-dollar bill on the classroom bulletin board one Monday morning and informed the class (a very challenging group of high school students) that he would take down that same twenty-dollar bill on Friday afternoon. The gamble worked- he trusted the students and they honored that trust by leaving the money tacked to the bulletin board. Confronted by a student as to why he would have taken such a chance, Riffle responded, "You guys are my friends and you don't steal from your friends."

The heart of the book lies in the dozens of short anecdotal accounts about former students. These captivating stories celebrate many success stories of special education students. In addition, Riffle also addresses the many real issues teachers must face with students such as drugs, poverty, depression, and death.

Every teacher says at some point in his career, "With all I've seen and heard, I could write a book." Well, here it is. Riffle has taken the time to do what all teachers have promised to do at one time or another- write a book! I'm certain you'll find as much enjoyment in reading his book as Pete did in reliving those thirty-seven years as he wrote the book.

Gerald Achenbach, Ed.D.

Friend and Fellow Educator

All children who walk into your classroom have a story:

Listen to them and it will be read to you;

Befriend them and be part of a new chapter;

Teach them and help author their dreams.

Peter W. Riffle

CHAPTER 1

"Why can't I learn like everyone else?"

...the author

From my earliest days in school, I still remember the fear of being ridiculed and feeling out of place with other kids. I would try to read and comprehend what was in a book, but most often printed words made no sense to me. Attempting to pronounce words correctly was also a constant struggle and source of embarrassment. I discovered at an early age that if a teacher would call on other students about information found in the reading, I could usually absorb enough material to fake comprehension. If that method didn't work, I simply told the teacher I wasn't paying attention. I spent many recesses inside, but my personal secret was never exposed; it was better to be miserable than ashamed. My time to shine in class occurred when the teacher lectured on subject matter. *That* was how I learned.

I always felt stupid compared to my classmates. Why couldn't I read and spell? My spelling was so atrocious that I made a joke out of it with my teachers and friends. In fact, my high school counselor described me as "a happy-go-lucky kid." How wrong he was! The truth of the matter is that no one ever really knew how unhappy I was. My high school yearbook reinforced the charade. Any posed photograph of me was so misleading because I had this ridiculously wide smile on my face. I vividly recall grinning that way so people would think that I *was* happy and carefree.

One asset I possessed was my memory. Anything learned by heart I retained. My high school Spanish teacher used to assign 400 vocabulary words for a unit test. I would sit down and, within a short period of time, have every word memorized. I "aced" that type of test, bombed the rest, but still passed Spanish for the year. I've impressed my friends for years with my ability to remember phone numbers and birthdays. What a great talent. All that and fifty cents would get me a cup of coffee!

Since I come from a family of educators, entering the field of teaching seemed like a natural thing to do. Even when I was young, the desire to be a teacher was strong because I had been inspired by my mother, who was an outstanding educator, and also by my sixth grade teacher, Mr. Paul Grebinger. But how could I get into college with my grades? Fortunately, my brother Paul stepped in to help me. He was a Navy veteran and a sophomore at Kutztown State College (now Kutztown University) in Pennsylvania. He used his influence plus my athletic ability to help me get accepted into school.

In college I considered myself an academic misfit. *How was I to compete with all of these smart kids?* The four years spent at Kutztown were filled with anxiety, but I willed myself to succeed. Cutting classes was never an option because I knew if I could hear the professors say it, I could understand it. My roommate was a lifelong friend whose scholastic ability demoralized me. I stayed in my room and studied while he went out and shot hoops or did whatever else he wanted to do, yet he received grades considerably better than mine. I was so sure I would flunk out I never bought anything with the college's name on it, not even a notebook. I didn't want anything lying around to remind me that I was a failure. Talk about being a "fish out of water!" Yet despite a constant uphill struggle, I persevered.

Early in my college career I had to choose an education major and this obligation created a real dilemma. I convinced myself I wasn't intelligent enough to teach regular education students, and, if I did, they would surely find out how stupid I was. The choice became simple – Special Education for the Visually Impaired. All of my students would be blind or severely visually challenged, and I figured their disability would balance out my own problem.

Nevertheless, I still had to register for a freshmen English composition course because it was a basic curriculum requirement for all students. Wrestling with my self-doubts again, I went into the professor's office three times a week and wrote practice essays that were probably horrendous. After the final exam, he called me into his office. He didn't mince words. "I guess you know you failed my course." I was devastated – all that effort for nothing and the word "failed" dogging me again. Observing my crestfallen face, he quickly added, "But in all my years of teaching, I have never taught a student who worked so hard, and for this effort I'm giving you a C for the course."

Following my freshman year I was on academic probation; in fact, my advisor called me in and told me to enlist in the Army. (Now there's a real confidence builder!) That summer I took a psychology course from one of the college's senior professors. It was a struggle from the beginning with so much to read and comprehend. I tried, but, as usual, I couldn't understand what I was reading. At the conclusion of the course, this professor also called me into his office. He told me he saw something special in me and thought I could become an outstanding teacher. I was totally shocked when he confided he was giving me a B for the course!

The two gifts given to me by those professors got me off probation and on my way to becoming a teacher. I'm sure neither one of them thought too much about what they did, but they changed my entire life. The help that they gave me has never been a secret. I have related this story to many people, including my students. I frequently think of these two men and am still sincerely thankful for their faith in me.

When I signed up for a psychology course for the fall semester of my sophomore year, I little suspected the importance of that decision. A new professor, Dr. Constance P. Dent, was assigned to teach that class. Almost immediately I became enthralled by her stimulating lectures. She was a consummate professional, and her office door was always open to her students. I spent many hours over the next three years in that office learning a great deal about psychology, but even more about people and life. She taught me to tolerate individual differences and to look for the underlying reasons why children act or react a certain way.

In October 1996, the Women's Counseling Service of Berks County, Pennsylvania, held a testimonial dinner to honor Dr. Dent for her dedicated commitment to her profession. She was allowed to bring a former student with her as a special guest, and she selected me. I just kept thinking, *Of all the outstanding academic students she has had over all the years, she chose me!* As I rose to speak that night, I felt prouder than I had ever felt before. There are not enough words in our language to express my gratitude for what she has meant to me.

Finally – in January of my senior year – I experienced the giddy realization that I was going to graduate and allowed myself the luxury of buying a class ring, the only item I ever purchased with Kutztown's name on it. I had earned my degree in four years with a QPA of 2.26 – not great, but enough to bring me much closer to my goal.

My first teaching position was with the office of the Berks County Superintendent of Schools in Reading, Pennsylvania. I'll never forget the thrill of my interview because it meant that my lifelong dream was about to come true. The special education supervisor and her assistant questioned me at length about my teaching philosophy. An hour later they told me the job was mine. To say the least, I was ecstatic.

Then they asked me if I had any further concerns about the job. From their quizzical looks I knew something was amiss, but, for the life of me, I couldn't think what it might be. *Oh, God! What did I forget to ask them?* I was certain I could somehow still "flunk" this interview. Finally the superintendent smiled and said, "Don't you want to know how much you're going to be earning?" Truthfully, I was so excited about becoming a teacher that my future salary didn't even matter.

I worked as an itinerant teacher of visually impaired children for three years. Just prior to my first school year, I became totally blind in my left eye due to an injury. Ironic, wasn't it? *I chose to become a teacher of visually impaired youngsters and then lost my sight in one eye.*

Susie

One of my very first days as a young teacher took me to a kindergarten class in a small rural school. All itinerant teachers at that time worked with their children in any space available, usually a guidance office. As I waited for this little girl, excitement at the prospect of teaching began to mount.

When the teacher brought Susie into the office, the little moppet took one look at me and started crying. Between sobs she begged to go back to her classroom. The teacher and I had no other choice until we could figure out what was wrong. They walked quickly out of the room leaving me puzzled and disheartened.

The teacher soon came back with a smile on her face and revealed that Susie didn't want to work with me because I was so tall. We both laughed about that, and I agreed it was possibly a frightening situation to be 3'6" and have a teacher towering three feet above you.

The next time I saw Susie I was sitting down on one of those little kindergarten-size chairs so I would be closer to her height. Showing no signs of fear, she walked into the room and we proceeded to have a very nice conversation. We met twice a week thereafter and really got along quite well.

A few weeks later her teacher told me to make sure that I didn't miss our next session. I asked why, but she only smiled and said, "You'll see; just be here."

The next time we met, little Susie confidently took me by the hand and led me back to her classroom. She guided me to the front of the room and proudly announced, "This is my big friend, Mr. Riffle, and he's what I brought for *show-and-tell* today." Imagine my surprise at being an object for display! Some of the little kids took turns standing next to me to see how tall I was while the amused building principal and the grinning teacher stood in the back of the room. I was informed I had the dubious distinction of being the school's first human selected for a show-and-tell presentation. To be perfectly honest, I loved it because Susie and I had bonded.

Elaine

I first met Elaine when I was a new teacher of the visually impaired in the 1968-69 school year. She was in tenth grade at the time and was a very likeable young woman. My supervisor called me in to talk about Elaine's condition. I was told she had degeneration of the retinas and would probably be blind within a few short years. My responsibility was to teach her how to cross a street, use a cane, and read Braille without letting her know the prognosis of her disease.

Elaine knew her sight was deteriorating but did not realize the severity of her disease. We talked at great length about her eyes, and I tactfully suggested that just in case the worst might happen, I would teach her a few things to help her cope with any unforeseen difficulties.

As I now look back on that situation, I can not believe this responsibility was placed on such a young, inexperienced teacher. Elaine is now legally blind but does have some functional sight. I still speak with her every few years; she is happily married and has three small children.

The students I worked with as an itinerant teacher were great kids, but I wanted a classroom of my own. A major drawback was driving forty to fifty miles a day, making me feel eligible for membership in the Teamsters Union! I was spending as much time driving as I was teaching. Three years later I became certified in teaching mentally impaired students.

After being hired to teach at a suburban school near Reading, Pennsylvania, I realized almost instantly that I had found my educational niche. I loved these kids and felt comfortable with them. It's embarrassing to admit now, but I figured that with their learning difficulties, they would never realize that I, too, had a problem. My biggest fear was that another faculty member might somehow uncover my "secret." I still believed I didn't have the necessary intelligence to teach.

When my supervisor took me into the high school to show me my classroom, I was very upset. For starters, the room was pink. I remember thinking about that color for a moment: *I have emotional support students who will be spending the large portion of their day in a pink room. Why not feed them sugar cubes too!*

The classroom was filled with woodworking tools plus all kinds of arts and craft material. I implored the supervisor to have the room painted a soft pastel blue and to remove all of those "playground" supplies. I guaranteed him if my kids wanted to take woodshop or art, they would do it in regular classes. He asked me if I was positive I wanted to do that; I assured him that was exactly what I wanted. I told him this was a classroom and would be run that way. I also informed him that the subject matter taught in this classroom would parallel the regular education program. He smiled and said, "Lots of luck."

When I first started teaching, little distinction was made between the various types of learning disabilities. All kids – with dissimilar disabilities – were put in one class; hence, there were life skills, learning disabilities, emotional support, mentally retarded, physically impaired and multi-disabled children all in the same room. This impossible teaching situation created some "interesting" days. Many times a special education teacher was in a survival mode for most of the school year. I frequently encouraged the LD and ES kids to help their fellow classmates because I would have as many as thirty diverse students in one class by myself!

The former role of a special education teacher basically consisted of keeping the students under control and out of everyone else's hair. My room was at the end of a remote hallway and not near any other classroom. Frankly, I was happy to be isolated. The gentleman who supervised my class didn't know any more about special education than I knew about open-heart surgery. Fortunately, he was a great guy who never pretended to know my field and supported me in anything I did.

When I went searching for teaching material in my classroom, I found only some outdated math and reading books from the elementary schools. In the early Seventies very few textbooks were published for special education students. I became a scavenger right before school started and confiscated some discarded biology and American history books that I adapted for my classes. I used to compare my situation to the old Christmas story, the "Island of Misfit Toys." For many years that's what we felt like. Today there are many catalogs from which special education teachers can select interesting and appropriate material.

My first week of teaching in my own classroom was one I will never forget. Two teachers had resigned the year before rather than teach my kids. One woman had even put her desk cater-cornered so they couldn't get behind her! Comprising part of this infamous class were five students on parole, including one charged with assault and battery. I was walking into a real challenging situation. My mother, an experienced teacher, always warned me: *Never make a threat that you don't intend to carry out*. I took that bit of wisdom with me as I entered the "combat zone."

My first two days of teaching on the "front line" dispelled any previous notion that teaching was always a noble and glorious profession. Standing stiffly at the front of the classroom, I attempted to follow the carefully prepared lesson plans. I began to speak, but the students ignored me and talked to each other instead. Here was a 6'6", 240-pound man who suddenly felt invisible. I continued to fire off volleys of vital information, but my educational artillery was useless; the students were entrenched in their foxholes, and I was their enemy.

Battle fatigue set in early. In retreat Thursday night, I considered any possible tactical errors I may have committed, but that was a fruitless endeavor. A new battle plan had to be drawn up. Some radical and unorthodox strategy was needed to get their attention. Unlike my predecessors, I was determined not to run up the white flag. I had come too far.

Friday morning arrived. Armed only with my new D-Day mentality, I marched into school ready to engage their minds. At precisely eight o'clock I purposely allowed all the kids to enter the room before I did and then locked the door with a loud click behind us.

After securing the door, I yanked the shade down and strode to my desk. As anticipated, most of the kids were warily watching me. Slowly and deliberately I took off my sport coat and hung it carefully over my chair. Standing in front of them with arms folded across my chest, I said in a controlled voice, "Okay, you sons-of-bitches, we're now going to find out who's in charge of this class!"

Let me emphasize that I definitely do not condone using profanity in the classroom, but for the first time this unruly student regiment snapped to attention. In a low tone I outlined the next conditions: "We're going to slug it out, and the winner runs the classroom; but I must warn you when the fight starts, it will be man-to-man, not teacher-against-student." I scanned their faces intently and abruptly asked, "Who wants to be first?" The shell-shocked students just sat there in stunned silenced. Thank God, no one stood up!

Assuming a more conciliatory stance, I calmly continued. "Now it's been settled; I'm in charge of this class. The next thing I want you to know is that the only reason I'm here is to help you, and, if you give me half a chance, that's exactly what I'll do." It was a major professional gamble, not one I would necessarily recommend today, but it worked. The attitude-adjustment bomb had been dropped and there were no casualties. I never had any more trouble with this group. As they say in the old gangster movies, I had "made my bones."

A remarkable postscript to this story unfolded later that year after I bought a farmhouse that needed a lot of repairs. These same kids, armed only with energy and enthusiasm, came up to the farm on weekends and worked quite a few hours for me. I remember telling them that I could not afford to pay them, and the one boy said, "Don't worry about that, Mr. Riffle. You help us during the week, and we'll help you on weekends."

Their hard labor didn't go entirely unrewarded. They were provided with hotdogs and hamburgers on the grill and the enjoyment of each other's company. The only rule I enforced was, *No smoking in the house.* Frequently while working with these kids, I wondered what their previous teachers might have said if they could have witnessed this scene. These "delinquents" just wanted someone to care about them.

Many years later during an open house at school, one of my boys from that first class walked in with his wife. I hadn't seen him in about twenty years, but I recognized him immediately. I warmly shook Mike's hand, and he introduced me to his wife. Out of curiosity, I asked her if she had ever heard the story about that startling impression I had made on Mike and his friends. She told me that Mike had mentioned me throughout their married life and that the only reason for coming to open house that night was to see me.

As the years passed, I knew without any doubt that teaching these kids was what God had put me on this earth to accomplish. I loved being with them; they made me feel special, never inadequate. I always accepted their disabilities, and they were never critical of my "unexposed" shortcomings. Definitely all was right with the world, or at least with my classroom. Ironically, all my own learning insecurities were about to surface again.

Sometime around my twenty-first year of teaching, my supervisor told me I was going to have an instructional assistant in my room. This person's name was Elaine and she was a certified English teacher. I hit the roof! Protesting vehemently, I told him, "I've taught all these years, and I don't need an assistant. Furthermore, I don't want one!" He looked me straight in the eye and said, "I didn't ask you if you want her; I'm telling you you're getting her!"

So unnerving was this prospect, I considered quitting rather than being embarrassed in front of this woman. I couldn't sleep for weeks before school started. I remember thinking how mortified I'd be the first time this "assistant" corrected my spelling or a mispronounced word. The first few days she was in my classroom, I felt like I was standing naked in front of her!

Gradually I began to relax. Her demeanor and her pleasant personality put me at ease; she never once commented on any of my language errors. As time progressed we became a team and have worked together for many years. She has become my personal dictionary and spell-checker.

Not many years ago I was attending a monthly staff meeting when my supervisor put a basic list of learning disabilities on the overhead projector. I had seen this list a hundred times but never really concentrated on what was included. As I read down the list, I whispered under my breath, "My God, that's me!" This belated revelation was a shock to my system, but things finally started to make sense. *I was teaching learning-disabled students and only now realizing I was also learning-disabled.* No one had any idea how happy that made me.

The next day in school I told all my students that I was also learning-disabled just like they were. And while I told them my entire life story, disbelief registered on their faces. We started comparing personal experiences, and I knew exactly what they were talking about. Every year before the students have their first lesson in my classroom, I confide in them about my learning disability. I've overheard many of them tell other students "he's one of us." Knowing that I have a disability has given me a great deal of insight into how my students think and feel.

Mindy

When a blind student named Mindy first entered my classroom, she captured my heart with her sweet personality and her cute giggle. The only thing about Mindy that worked on my nerves was her affiliation with a certain football team; she and her family were diehard Dallas Cowboy fans. In fact, frequently the day after my beloved Eagles lost a game, she had the audacity to bring me a sympathy gift. I used to threaten her with summer school, but she just laughed at me.

One day she was sitting at her desk looking uncharacteristically downcast. I walked up to her and asked her what was wrong. She admitted she *was* sad because she saw a lot of dark clouds in her mind. Without saying a word I threw my arms around her and started hugging her. She began to laugh instantly. When I stopped, she smiled and said, "There are still a few clouds left." I hugged her again, harder. She laughed so much she was crying. Between lingering giggles she told me the clouds were gone and that I was now her "cloud chaser."

That phrase immediately caught my attention. I knelt next to her, put my hand on her shoulder, and softly said, "Mindy, Mr. Riffle is toying with the idea of writing a book, and if he ever does, he's going to name it *The Cloud Chaser*." Here is that book, Mindy – and it's dedicated to you!

CHAPTER **2**

*"You know, God didn't lay many smarts on me,
so I don't know what I'm going to do in life."*
...spoken by a learning-disabled child

Before delving further into this book, the reader should be advised that *The Cloud Chaser* has not evolved from extensive research conducted at one of our country's finer universities, nor does it offer an unending litany of statistics amassed from nationwide surveys. The opinions expressed within these pages are mine and mine alone. Having spent more than thirty-seven years in the "trenches" and a lifetime being learning-disabled, I feel reasonably qualified to give the reader a unique perspective on learning disabilities – a view from both sides of the desk. Therefore, if this book was purchased to discover a new clinical approach for teaching or working with these children, put it down now, or simply use *The Cloud Chaser* as a doorstop or a large coaster!

Most people do not truly understand learning disabilities – disorders that damage or interfere with a child's ability to learn. In fact, there are even some teachers who question their actual existence. This skepticism probably stems from the fact that children with learning disabilities frequently have average or above-average intelligence and have normal vision and hearing. There are often no discernible physical traits to suggest a learning problem. Therefore, these young people will walk into and out of regular education classes all day long without most teachers being aware of their learning problems. Instead, they may simply view these students as lazy underachievers.

What, then, is a learning-disabled child? Scientists believe that learning disabilities result from minimal damage to the brain or to major nerves leading to the brain. Once this occurs – whether before, during, or after birth – the information transmitted by the senses to the brain is not accurately conveyed, creating a favorable condition for the weakened development of such basic skills as concentration, coordination, language, and memory. These deficiencies ultimately affect speaking, understanding language, reading, spelling, math, and behavior. The stage is thus set for poor academic performance in school.

By some estimates, as many as 10 percent of school-age children have one or more learning disabilities. Symptoms indicative of a learning disability may not be recognized early in a child's life. Only after formal education has begun do certain learning patterns start to emerge. The importance of the teacher's role in detecting these problems cannot be overemphasized because early diagnosis is critical. Specific teaching methods can be implemented to aid many students overcome their handicaps and experience success in school. Otherwise, their lives might be adversely affected. Children identified later in life tend to develop inferiority complexes or unhealthy coping mechanisms, or simply want to give up after years of failure.

Emmitt

Emmitt was one of my students whose delayed diagnosis clearly exemplifies the seriousness of learning disabilities continuing into adulthood. When Emmitt was in high school, he enrolled in every remedial reading class offered in order to help himself become a better reader. However, Emmitt's disability was so severe by this late stage that only limited improvement could be observed. Following high school, he doggedly pursued his quest to improve his reading, but to little avail; he was still being tutored when he was in his late twenties. I frequently encouraged him to get past this disappointment and to concentrate on his strong points. But to Emmitt, only the ability to read gave you a credible claim to being an intelligent person, and nothing I said could convince him otherwise.

The only person who provided any emotional stability in his life was his mother. Tragically, she died when he was twenty-seven years old. Following his mother's death, Emmitt sank into a deep depression. To add to his problems, his co-workers constantly mocked him because he couldn't read. They badgered him daily, never allowing him any respite from their ridicule. They played cruel "jokes" on Emmitt, such as telling him to read a work order and then making fun of him when he failed.

One day there was a knock at my classroom door. There stood Emmitt looking gaunt and miserable. Dark circles shadowed his red eyes, indicating he hadn't slept well in weeks. Urgently, he beckoned me out into the hallway and told me he needed to talk to me immediately. Once we were seated in an empty classroom, Emmitt blurted, "Mr. Riffle, you're going to be very mad at me." In a puzzled voice, I asked him to explain what was wrong. He opened his shirt, showed me the bandages, and then confided he had shot himself the week before. Fortunately, the bullet had hit his sternum and then had ricocheted out through his right shoulder. Granted, this is an extreme reaction to having a learning disability, but always feeling badly about oneself can eventually erode self-esteem and lead to serious – even tragic – consequences.

• • • • •

After this unnerving experience with Emmitt, I resolved that one of the first things on my agenda at the beginning of each year would be to educate the new students about learning disabilities. When I introduce this discussion, I particularly stress one point: Having a learning disability doesn't mean you are not intelligent. The one trait so prevalent among new students is thinking that they are *dumb* or *stupid*. I warn my students that those two words are not allowed in my classroom when referring to themselves or to other classmates. I do confess to them that I still frequently belittle myself because after all these years of feeling inferior, it's a difficult habit to break. After this candid revelation, I have their undivided attention as I relate my own frustrating and embarrassing moments when my personal disabilities put me at a disadvantage.

One major characteristic of a learning-disabled person is poor reading comprehension. For me to read instructions on how to put a child's Christmas toy together is wasted time. Fortunately, I have excellent mechanical aptitude because relying on written directions to construct something is a distinct drawback to an otherwise pleasurable activity. What I have always depended upon is looking at the pictures and the parts and then figuring out the assembly process in my head.

Years ago I used to build recreation rooms as a summer job. I specifically remember one job that required the installation of bifold doors. I told my workers to take a break so I could figure out how to do it. One of my men said, "Pete, aren't you going to read the directions?" I replied, "No, directions are written by fools for fools, and I ain't no fool." The truth is that I can't comprehend them very well, and they did make me feel like the fool.

Perceptual disorders interfere with the brain's ability to organize and interpret sights and sounds. When I look at multisyllabic words, I don't see what a person without a learning disability sees. For example, take the word "comfortable." When I look at this word, the first thing I see is "fort." I have done this my entire life when reading. Moreover, even being aware of this habit doesn't prevent me from doing it. Some children having perceptual problems are unable to ascertain at what point one word ends and another begins.

Pronouncing words correctly is also extremely difficult for me; I cringe when reading in public. Words that would be simple for anyone else to read are next to impossible for me. My minister once invited me to read scripture during the church service; I told him I wouldn't do the reading, but would be willing to preach a sermon. He had an amazed look on his face after hearing that response!

For twenty years I was the timer/announcer at high school wrestling matches. Before each match I would have the opposing team's scorekeeper give me the pronunciation of each wrestler's name. Sometimes that wouldn't help, but I quickly learned to invent methods to cover up my inadequacies. In this particular situation, I always introduced our wrestler first, and then while the crowd was applauding, rapidly slurred the other kid's name. Certain wrestlers from other schools turned and looked at me as if to say, "What the heck did you say my name was?"

Another problem I've encountered my entire life is recording spoken numbers. I vividly remember my seventh-grade math teacher reciting a list of numbers we were to write down. I was in a nervous sweat over completing this task, so I had to figure out a way to slow her down. When she said the next number, I yelled, "Bingo!" She stopped, and everyone laughed, but I didn't even crack a smile because I was too busy finishing up my paper.

I have been frequently embarrassed when someone is giving me a phone number to copy down. I need to have it repeated several times. Ironically, once I commit a phone number to memory, I never forget it. For example, I wanted to call a friend I had lost contact with over the years. I went to the phone and dialed the number I hadn't called in five or six years, yet remembered. Some learning-disabled students have great difficulty taking notes in class; they hear what is being said, but their brains can't process the information as quickly as those of "normal" people can. Children who have a disability that affects their memory are not able to recall a series of instructions or learn a sequence, such as the alphabet or a telephone number.

Poor spelling can be another indicator of a learning-disabled child. The many times I've been embarrassed by this aspect of my disability are certainly too numerous to recount, but one incident, which happened a few years after I was out of college, is branded into my memory. I had taken our new kitten to the vet for a checkup. When it was time to pay, the receptionist informed me the bill was twelve dollars. I clutched my checkbook and froze: I couldn't spell "twelve!" I can still recall the burning sense of shame that overwhelmed me.

I panicked. In my mind, all eyes in the room were on "this dumb man who can't spell." I tried to make light of it while I was dying inside. I told the woman I couldn't remember how to spell "twelve." Before she could assist me, another woman in the waiting room piped up, "Why don't you write out a check for ten dollars and then give her two dollars out of your wallet?" At that moment, I wanted to drop off the face of the earth. The receptionist kindly helped me write out the check.

Then I had to mortify myself further by turning around and facing the other people seated in the room. The few steps from the desk to the door seemed endless. When I slumped into my car, the rear-view mirror reflected my crimson countenance and I began to beat myself up emotionally: *How could I be so stupid? Here I was – a college graduate – a teacher – and I couldn't spell a simple word.* That night I sat down and repeated t-w-e-l-v-e over and over until I had it memorized. I wouldn't be embarrassed again – at least not by that word.

Although learning disabilities have put me at a disadvantage all my life, the one advantage it has afforded me is understanding the daily frustration that most of my students encounter in the classroom. I stress to my students that having a learning disability is no one's fault because often they want to blame their parents. However, in my opinion, children feeling "stupid" or "dumb" as a result of their learning problems have been influenced by two major sources – parents and teachers. The guilt might not be intentional, but that unwelcome message is often conveyed by words, gestures, or even facial expressions. Children easily spot displeasure when they can't perform certain tasks, so handling situations with sensitivity is vital

When working with learning-disabled students, I have observed patterns of behavior that are a direct result of their feelings of inadequacy and have tried – whenever possible – to avoid situations that accentuate their weaknesses. For instance, many kids will periodically glance at the other students in the classroom while taking a test. They're not watching in order to cheat on the test; they're watching so they can hand in their tests along with everyone else. Rather than feel academically inferior to their classmates, they will purposely sacrifice a better grade just to hand in their tests at the "appropriate" time. A resultant rule I have in class: All papers will be collected at the end of the class period. This cuts down on students worrying about looking stupid because they are taking longer to complete the test or assignment.

Another problem facing those of us with learning disabilities is the inability to move easily from line to line in any given text. As our eyes move down to the next line to be read, we lose our place. When I was a child, the teacher smacked you with a ruler if you used your finger to keep your place. To avoid the unwanted wooden reminder, I cleverly used my pencil point instead of my finger to help me stay on the correct line. It worked because the teachers never realized what I was doing. I encourage my students to use their fingers or an index card to visually guide them while reading.

Teachers should pay very close attention to students who struggle excessively with note taking. Copying down notes as a teacher speaks is next to impossible for some learning-disabled kids. They hear a teacher's voice and understand, but can't seem to process the information from their brains to their hands. Hoping to fool everyone, they will move their pencils across the paper, pretending to write everything down. Periodically – especially in the beginning of the year – a teacher should check notebooks. Learning-disabled kids are great fakers; they will do whatever is necessary to fit in with their peers.

During a class lecture, putting important material on the board or on an overhead projector is immensely helpful. However, taking notes even this way can be a difficult task for some students. Looking up at the board and then looking back down at their notebooks can be a confusing process. Once again perceptual disorders can prevent the eyes from easily making these adjustments. Another beneficial aid is to always present printed material. Writing in cursive will cause most students to spend too much time trying to decipher a teacher's handwriting.

One major aspect concerning the learning-disabled population that is rarely discussed is the burden of shame they secretly bear. Even now – as a grown adult – I use coping techniques to avoid looking foolish in front of other people. For example, if I'm in a meeting where I am required to read the same paper other people are reading, I will sit back and wait a few moments before I start. This maneuver prevents me from uselessly trying to finish reading when everyone else does. If I start reading the material at the same time, I will be more concerned with stopping when the others do rather than with focusing on the information.

Discussing these cover-ups with my students, I have found that they use similar techniques to "protect" themselves in comparable situations. Over the years, I've had numerous kids who have gone to great lengths to keep their disabilities secret. It's almost as bad as if they had robbed a bank and are afraid of being caught. Because I understand their sensitivities, I sometimes find myself aiding and abetting my students with this deception. When regular education students ask me what I teach, I tell them history and economics. This response might be lying by omission because I teach learning support history and economics.

Donna

When the morning bell rang to signal the start of my first day of teaching, an attractive young woman walked into my classroom and introduced herself as Donna. She was the very first student to enter my classroom, and, after all these many years, she is still one of my all-time favorites. I soon discovered that Donna had a severe reading disability and couldn't spell even simple words. She struggled all through school with this disability. She was as intelligent as anyone else, but she didn't view herself that way.

When I first met Donna's fiancé, he asked me what courses I teach. Donna's eyes widened at the fearful prospect that I would say "special education." Instantly sensing her alarm, I told him I teach 19th and 20th Century American History. As previously mentioned, I was afraid a co-worker might find out about my own disability, and therefore didn't want an aide or anyone else in my room; no one could know about my problem. Donna's secret was safe with me.

As often as I've tried to reassure Donna that she shouldn't feel ashamed of her problem, she is still adamant about keeping her disability a secret. In 1998, the Learning Channel was considering featuring me on one of their programs. The producers requested a list of former students and their phone numbers so they could be questioned about their experiences in my classroom. Donna refused to be interviewed in person and granted them a phone conversation only as long as she didn't have to divulge her last name. I know while I'm writing this page that she will request I use a pseudonym for her in this book.

Bonnie

Bonnie was so adept at making herself disappear that she should have been in magic shows. She refined the act of sneaking into and out of my classroom without being seen by other students into an art form. She sat right next to the door, but positioned herself in such a way that no one could see her from the hallway. When the bell rang, she vanished out the door in a flash to avoid being seen exiting a special ed. classroom. She was very friendly and polite, but would avoid saying hello to me in the hallway: After all, I was a special ed. teacher! I tried to counsel her as I had Donna, but to no avail.

Mike

Many of my learning-disabled kids build thick emotional walls around themselves for protection. Mike was just that sort of person: He never let any of us into his world – until one rainy night his senior year.

He was a starting cornerback for our varsity football team, and we were playing for the league championship. The game took place in a torrential downpour. When an opposing player caught the winning pass in front of Mike as time expired, he was devastated.

I left the stands and stood in the end zone, hoping to see him when he left the field. As the team was walking to the locker room, he spied me and trudged my way. He put his arms around me and cried. Being a former athlete, I did what I could to comfort him. While talking to him, I noticed he never released his grip.

This was the first time I had ever seen the "real" Mike. He and I talked about that night the following week. I told him there was nothing wrong with displaying emotion, and that it certainly didn't make him less of a man. So many young men are caught up in a faulty notion: If I show emotion, I'm a "wimp."

Later that year, Mike began working with one of my physically challenged students, and it was beneficial to both of them. Now that his protective stone wall had crumbled, he was able to talk about his disability, and, with a newfound confidence, realized he could help others as well. There is not always a cure for a disability, but learning how to cope with one is part of the adjustment process.

Before some students reach this stage, they may handle their disabilities in an undesirable manner. Students diagnosed at a later stage will more likely fit into one of these three categories: *an inordinately quiet student, a belligerent troublemaker*, or *the class clown*. But no matter which of these three behaviors they exhibit, the same purpose is served: the disability is disguised.

The quiet, withdrawn student is frequently – but not always – a young woman. This person follows the premise: *If I don't say anything, no one can make fun of me.*

Janet

I suppose the phrase "quiet as a church mouse" is appropriate when describing Janet. One thing that always works on my nerves is when kids will not interact with me. When I posed questions to Janet, she would remain mute, barely shaking or nodding her head to indicate *yes* or *no*. Sometimes she just shrugged her shoulders if she wasn't sure of the answer. I tried to gently encourage her to respond orally, but Janet didn't seem to possess vocal chords!

One day while walking past her desk, I tapped her shoulder and said, "You're IT."

She looked up at me in surprise and said, "What?"

I explained, "We're playing tag, and you're IT."

She touched the kid next to her and said, "You're IT." It was a breakthrough but still not directed at me.

I then informed her, "Only you and I are in the game."

She touched my arm when I walked past her and said again, "You're IT."

"Sorry," I replied, "I'm on base." As you might have guessed, she was always IT because no matter where I was, I was on base. This silly little game broke the ice between us.

As the year progressed, Janet became more comfortable with her teachers, even to the point of doling out hugs every day when she came to school and every day when she left school. Watching her confidently interact with her peers and the staff always brought a smile to my face.

Two or three years after she graduated, I was at a local food store when I felt someone touch my shoulder and say, "You're IT!" I turned around and there was Janet. I hugged her and said, "Sorry, I'm on base." We both laughed and she protested, "You've always cheated!"

Why I started playing tag is still a mystery to me. I do so many strange things like that, and sometimes I get results I never expected. If that hadn't worked, I would have tried something else.

• • • • •

The belligerent child presents an altogether different façade and is often difficult to handle in class. This student goes on the offensive and adopts the following approach: *Nobody's gonna mess with me or I'll cause such problems that everyone will leave me alone or throw me out of class.* These kids would rather be expelled from class than be made to look foolish in front of their peers.

Fred

When Fred was in tenth grade, the school was ready to permanently expel him. He was disruptive and disrespectful to students and staff alike. Our high school principal came to my room one day and asked me if I knew Fred. I recognized the name and had heard that he had been in lots of trouble, but I didn't actually know him. I was asked to consider taking him into my class, and was flatly told that if I didn't take him, he was gone for good. I've never turned a kid down, so I told the principal I'd give him a chance. It should be noted that Fred was later diagnosed as being learning-disabled.

A meeting was set up with the boy, his mother, a counselor, the school psychologist, the high school principal, and me. When I walked into the meeting, the only vacant chair was right next to Fred. While taking that seat, I looked at him and saw what I always call "the hard-guy look," a mask frequently donned by a scared kid. The counselor and the school psychologist were painting this rosy picture for Fred, and, to say the least, he wasn't buying it.

Our principal, a real "kids-are-first" type of guy and an excellent judge of character, said to me, "Why don't you tell Fred how you feel?"

Without hesitation, I leaned over and very "sweetly" said, "Now, Fred, when you come to my class, I'll do all I can to help you. If anyone picks on you, I'll protect you." I paused slightly, put my finger right in his face, changed my tone of voice and added, "But if you step one foot out of line with me, I'll kick your ass! Now do you understand where I'm coming from?"

His facial expression changed quickly. With bulging eyes, he quickly answered, "Yes, sir!"

What a changed boy Fred became! I don't think any adult had ever stood up to him in his entire life. His problems in school came to a halt and his grades improved.

One Monday when I came to school, Fred was waiting for me at my door. When I asked why he was in school so early, he revealed that he had run away from home on Saturday. We discussed his situation privately, and I convinced him to return to his home with me.

When we walked into the house, he and his mother started screaming at each other. I stopped them from yelling for a moment and asked both if they loved each other. Reluctantly, they nodded their heads, so I said, "Okay, no more yelling; let's talk this out." It took a while, but they did settle their differences. By the time I left their house, mother and son were embracing each other.

Ultimately, Fred graduated from high school and then successfully completed a two-year trade school program to become a diesel mechanic. He has always hated school, but his current job requires him to go back to school at least twice a year. In addition to a good job and a beautiful home, he is also married and the father of three young children. When I talked to him not too long ago, he told me his kids were driving him crazy. I looked at him, smiled, and wryly remarked,

"This is what they call *payback*." He laughed and told me that's what his mother said, too.

Sharon

Sharon was a tall, thin young woman who had an intense *I-don't-take-crap-from-nobody* attitude. She and I got along pretty well, but I knew I had a tiger on my hands. One day when I was absent from school, a substitute teacher found out exactly what Sharon's "stripes" looked like!

While the students were working, the woman started searching through my center desk drawer, which my students know is off-limits. Sharon warned her not to look through my center drawer because "that's Mr. Riffle's personal stuff." The substitute told Sharon that because she was a teacher, she could do as she pleased.

Reportedly, Sharon got up from her desk and started walking toward the front of the room. The teacher asked her what she was doing, and Sharon replied, "I'm going to go through your purse."

The teacher grabbed her purse and said, "Oh, no, you're not!"

Sharon retorted, "Fine! You stay out of his desk drawers, and I'll stay out of your purse!"

The substitute informed my principal that she would never come in for me again.

Fred and Sharon were really never any trouble while they were in my class. Both fit my earlier description of kids diagnosed late in their academic careers: Fred was first diagnosed in tenth grade while Sharon was diagnosed in ninth grade. People might think that these kids should have handled their frustration in another manner. Nevertheless, such behavior is often exhibited by kids who have been frequently ridiculed or have been the constant butt of someone's joke.

• • • • •

The third type of learning-disabled student is the "class clown," a category I clearly fit into during my years in school. Every teacher who ever had me as a student would certainly remember my zany sense of humor. I was never disrespectful, but was instead what you might call an "interesting child!"

My youngest son Luke was a nonreader until sixth grade. He, like his father, was the class clown. The old Sixties song about a clown laughing on the outside, but crying on the inside described Luke perfectly. His learning disability eroded his self-esteem, but like so many of these kids, he kept his lack of self-confidence hidden. I wish I could say that now, as a young man in his twenties, he has gotten over those feelings, but he hasn't. Some pain never goes away.

Luke was an outstanding wrestler, and, after one particularly hard match, won in dramatic fashion, he said to me, "It doesn't matter if I can read or not out there, does it?" That statement hurt me deeply as a father. When I got him home, I sat him down and discussed learning disabilities with him. He politely listened, but I could see in his eyes that he had his own thoughts on the subject.

The class clown is certainly no different from the quiet child or the belligerent child, in that all of these children utilize distractions to keep the teacher and their classmates away from the real problem. To be sure, not every child who exhibits these characteristics is learning-disabled. However, a student who fits into one of these categories and exhibits other telltale symptoms should be evaluated by the school psychologist.

It isn't very difficult for average classroom teachers to recognize possible indicators of an undiagnosed learning-disabled child if they know what to look for. Only formal testing by a team of specialists can formally identify a child, but regular classroom teachers must be cognizant of these factors in order to initiate the identification process.

The following list highlights possible warning signs of learning disabilities:

1. Inability to spell basic words that are age-group appropriate.

2. Poor oral reading.

3. Difficulty answering comprehension questions.

4. Inability to take good notes.

5. Functioning two or more years below grade level.

6. Difficulty with pronunciation or speech.

7. Distractibility and inability to concentrate.

8. Inability to behave properly.

9. Poor memory.

10. Left-right and other spatial disorientations

11. Unusual way of printing letters.

12. Behavior typical of a class clown, a belligerent child, or a quiet, withdrawn child.

Learning-disabled children find so many unique ways to disguise their disabilities, but the one trait that runs true to form for each one of them is feeling inferior to "normal" kids. Therefore, a major goal for all special education teachers is to improve these damaged self-images. By whatever method it takes, plant in them the seed of confidence, cultivate their talents, and watch these children blossom.

CHAPTER 3

To teach - to instruct, in order for a person to
learn a skill or acquire knowledge.

Webster's Dictionary

If the above definition included everything you would ever have to do as a teacher, your job would be a snap! I regret to inform you that your students will not sit in front of you every day and beg you to teach them a new concept. Another misunderstanding is that *you* will only teach *them*. I readily profess that, after thirty-seven years of teaching, I have learned as much from my students as they have learned from me.

Your first few weeks as a new teacher are filled with both excitement and apprehension. Even after all these years on the job, I'm still eager to begin each new school year. The anticipation of meeting new challenges and new students always inspires me. I vividly recall waiting for the first students to enter my classroom in 1968. As I stood facing the empty desks, I also remember murmuring, "What the heck have I gotten myself into?" Before I could answer my own panicky question, the kids arrived, my room came alive, and the dual education of teacher and students began. In this chapter, I will endeavor to offer some insightful guidelines for your first years of teaching.

When you begin your teaching career, choose your associates carefully. I know this sounds like parental advice, but it can have a lasting impact on your teaching philosophy. In every faculty, just as in every other workplace, there are "doom-and-gloom" individuals. I haven't been in a faculty room in years because I got sick and tired of hearing a few teachers denigrate kids every day. I am convinced that both negative and positive attitudes are contagious, so make sure you come into contact with the right one. If you believe all kids have a good side, you'll find it; but if you persist in being negative, that pleasant discovery will never happen. Be a positive person, and you'll enjoy teaching immensely. Conversely, the students will enjoy having you as their teacher.

I'll never forget a regular education teacher commenting about one of my students who was terminally ill. While helping this boy acquire his lunch in our cafeteria, the other teacher pulled me aside and said, "That kid's dying, isn't he?"

I replied, "Yes, his disease is terminal."

This teacher shocked me by exclaiming, "How can you work with a kid like that? He's dying! I could never do that; I don't know how you can deal with him!"

These remarks came from a person considered an exemplary teacher in his field. He is known to be creative and works very well with his college-bound students, yet he was repulsed by the thought of working with this seriously ill student. I didn't comment, but I clearly remember thinking *What would you have me do? Should I take this unfortunate kid into the desert and leave him there to die like in Biblical times?*

Another disparaging remark by a faculty member was directed my way while I was heading back to my classroom after lunch. As I walked past him in the hallway, he stopped me and said, "I need to talk to you. When are you going to be back in your room with your knuckleheads?" I was flabbergasted by his thoughtless name-calling and had a very terse conversation with this man.

Once when a regular education teacher learned my classroom was being relocated next to hers, she sped to our superintendent's office and literally jumped up and down objecting to a special education class in *her* wing. I learned about this incident from a secretary who watched the whole scene unfold. This teacher was pleasant when she saw me in the hall, but I was aware of her true feelings. Her reaction was like a person claiming not to be a racist, yet protesting against having a member of a different ethnic group as a neighbor.

A few weeks after winning the Disney American Teacher Award, I was with my family at a local restaurant. While waiting for our table, I saw one of my former high school coaches having dinner with his family. I approached them, exchanged the usual small talk, and then told him about the unbelievable honor I had won. His response was one I'll never forget: "How can you win that? You only teach special ed." He wasn't kidding; he was dead serious. I was stunned, then furious, then ultimately stung by his words. I turned and walked away thinking *I've known this man for over forty years, and this is what he thinks of me, my profession, and – worst of all – my students!*

These incidents, among others, expose a little secret that special education teachers discuss only among themselves: A few regular education colleagues don't accept us as bona fide teachers. Any regular education teacher who reads this sentence will deny it, but veteran special education teachers have invariably encountered this attitude at various times throughout their teaching careers.

No matter what biased views you encounter, developing a good working relationship with your regular education co-workers is still essential. Our educational staff is outstanding, and teachers have generally been very cooperative when dealing with my students. To strengthen this relationship, over the years I have shared some of my class projects with these colleagues. They have no idea what we do in our classes, and this insight lends credibility to both special ed. teachers and students.

You should also *create* opportunities where you can discuss special education classes with regular education students. I cannot stress enough the importance of making these students aware of the existence of learning disabilities, one of the most misunderstood classifications in the field of education today. Knowing full well the social structure of a school can sometimes imitate the law of the jungle where only the strong survive, I made it a personal crusade to speak about this subject in eleventh-grade health classes and twelfth-grade parenting classes. Learning-disabled students benefit by having peer advocates. My daughter Abby and her friends led the way championing the cause of my students. Hopefully, my lectures helped other students develop empathy for many of my kids and curtailed some of the inappropriate behavior directed toward them.

Cooperation from the regular education staff is even more apparent if it starts at the administrative level. I have worked for five different superintendents and seven different high school principals, and they have all been supporters of our kids and our program. Looking back, I now realize that many of these administrators were way ahead of their peers in advocating special education classes.

Today there are laws in place to bolster your programs, but if your administrators don't give you much more than "lip service," you will be fighting an uphill battle. I know of local school districts where three learning support teachers share one instructional assistant, an injustice to both the students and the staff. Every class should have at least one full-time aide, while emotional support and life skills classes need two or more aides.

Our high school employs eleven full-time teachers and twenty-one instructional assistants. Anyone fortunate enough to work in a school district such as ours is indeed very lucky. Realtors have told our administrators that families with special needs youngsters have moved into our district because of our special education staff's superb reputation. During one department meeting, our special education director teasingly told us to stop doing such an outstanding job because we were running out of classroom space!

And, finally, never underestimate the important rapport necessary with two other groups of employees who also do outstanding jobs in your building. What you want to know or what you need to help you in your room will often come from the secretaries and custodians. There's an old saying "sergeants run the army." Well, the secretaries and custodians run the school. They work very hard and deserve respect because without them the school would not function.

Even supposing that all essential groups help foster a smooth transition to the classroom, the educator still faces a daunting and demanding task. You must be more than just a human dispenser of facts. The special education teacher of the Twenty-first Century must also be prepared to assume the roles of psychologist, counselor, negotiator, banker (you will be surprised how much lunch money you will hand out), nurse, parent, and then teacher – when time permits!

The young teachers our colleges and universities are turning out today are much better trained than teachers of my generation. They are taught all of the newest techniques and methods to deal with special needs youngsters. They can write better individual education programs (I.E.P.) than I could ever hope to write. But I've always felt that special education teachers must be *special* people themselves. So many of the young people who sit in your classrooms will need your heart much more than your subject matter.

My son Matthew and his wife Diane are both trained in special education. They talk about new programs and concepts that are foreign to me. Needless to say, these new ideas are critical to the well-being of their students but should not overshadow the crucial qualities of love, understanding, respect, caring, and patience that are not taught in institutions of higher learning. I'm proud to say that both Matthew and Diane teach with their hearts, and the young people in their classrooms are privileged to have them as teachers.

I'm bothered a great deal when I hear young people state their intention to major in special education only to increase their likelihood of finding a job. Special ed. students have enough problems; they don't need a teacher who isn't totally dedicated to them. If this consideration is your principal reason for teaching special ed. students, please do these kids a favor and enter another field. It might be an old-fashioned opinion, but I believe that teaching special education is a calling.

What I consider a real loss is when young people who have an innate gift for teaching shy away from it for financial reasons. I certainly understand the importance of earning a good salary, but that shouldn't be the foremost consideration when choosing a career.

Brent and Byron

During the 1980s I had two brothers, Brent and Byron, who volunteered their tutoring skills in my classroom. They were two years apart in age, so for five years I had at least one of them with me. They were outstanding students who worked with my kids in a very caring way. These two young men were natural-born teachers, and my students were totally at ease with them. It can be a difficult situation to tutor within your peer group, but they fully mastered the task. When both of them graduated, they received our school's Altruism Award presented each year to a student who gives unselfishly to classmates. To my knowledge, they are the only two siblings to ever win this prestigious award.

I had harbored the hope that both of them would become teachers, but, instead, they became engineers. Brent told me he wanted to be an engineer because it was a much more lucrative profession than teaching. I realize money is important, but personal satisfaction at the end of the day is also a vital consideration when choosing a career. What a shame these two fine teaching prospects didn't become educators!

It is only natural to be concerned about the salary and the benefit package you will receive as a new teacher, but I would like to mention a major "bonus" you will receive if you merit it. This non-negotiable item is the affection your students will bestow upon you if you open your heart to them and demonstrate through your actions and words that you care about them as individuals. The stories about "Kara's concern" and "Jill's possessiveness" are just two of hundreds I could relate illustrating this point.

Kara

Kara, a.k.a. "Little Florence Nightingale," came to my rescue a few years ago. I had a pinched nerve in my neck that was extremely painful. Kara, who was in tenth grade at the time and wanted to pursue a career in health occupations, asked me what could be done to ease the pain. I told her the doctor recommended applying ice twice a day.

The next morning Kara came to class with an ice pack and a towel. She ordered me to ice down my neck twice daily for the rest of the school year. There were days when I protested that I didn't want the frosty therapy. Only half my size, she would plant herself in front of me with her hands on her hips, give me the "look" that I thought only mothers could confer, and scold, "Am I doing this for my own good or for yours?" Naturally, I relented and dutifully did as I was told. Kara and I had a lot of fun fussing over that ice pack.

Jill

Although I was in charge of a tenth-grade homeroom, I never seemed to have a pen to take attendance. A young woman named Jill sat next to my podium, and every morning I borrowed her pen to mark down absent students. One day, for some unknown reason, I borrowed a pen from another girl. As I turned to take attendance, I glanced at Jill. If "looks could kill," I wouldn't have been included in the roll call of the living! She just glared at me. On the way out of homeroom, I promised her that I would use her pen the rest of the year. She turned and peevishly replied, "Well, you don't have to use it if you don't want to!"

Using her pen every day had been of the utmost importance to Jill. I hadn't realized it at the time, but the pen had come to symbolize a bond between us. I guarantee you, for the rest of the year I used only Jill's pen to take roll. In fact, there was a touching ending to this story. The night she graduated, Jill ceremoniously presented me with a pen and pencil set.

The thoughtfulness and concern I have been privileged to receive from my students is indescribable. They always let me know that I am a special person in their lives. The irony is that they never seem to understand how truly special they are in my life. This is the type of reward that you won't see in your paycheck, but it is infinitely more precious than cold cash.

Although teaching can ultimately be very gratifying, establishing classroom discipline can be an initial drawback for the fledgling educator. Good classroom control does not depend on a teacher's physical size. Many of my co-workers, although small in stature, run a tight ship. Conversely, I've seen men as big as myself have absolute mayhem occurring in their classrooms. Well-managed classes depend upon the teacher displaying competence, confidence, and congeniality while being fair, firm, and consistent with classroom rules.

Paul

A young man named Paul who graduated from our school in the early 1980s was a big, tough, rugged kind of guy – a real outdoorsman. He excelled at welding at the career/technical center. In fact, he eventually became certified in underwater welding, a very dangerous occupation.

When Paul was in his early thirties, the welding teacher at career/tech underwent an appendectomy and had to be out of school for six weeks. The career/tech center contacted Paul to ask if he would consider substituting. He told me he had said, "Sure, how tough could it be?" He was about to find out!

Two weeks into his teaching assignment, he stopped in to see me. I could tell by his demeanor that something was amiss.

Frustrated, he said, "So help me, Mr. Riffle, I'm ready to kill some of those kids! How in God's name do you do it?"

I laughed. "What's the matter, Paul, not as easy on the other side of the desk as it looked?"

He threw up his hands and shook his head in despair. "Forget the other side of the desk; I'm talking about the other side of sanity! I wish I had been drafted instead!"

After Paul had finished airing his grievances, we sat down and I offered him some basic rules to foster better discipline. Having restocked his arsenal, he dubiously returned to the "front line." He contacted me a few days later to tell me that my suggestions had helped, but swore, "Once this hitch is over, I'm never going to reenlist!"

In my opinion, having classroom control correlates to mannerisms and how you handle disturbances. The first two or three weeks of school set the tone you want to have in your classroom. First of all, dress the part. Remember, you're a professional teacher; you're not out on a golf course. An old saying my late father related to football players holds true here: "Dress like a football player; you might fool someone into thinking you are one."

Be polite and courteous, but don't smile too much. Be stern when dealing with any behavior that is disrupting the learning process. Think before reacting to a classroom situation. Case in point: I grabbed a cigarette lighter from a boy one day, and, in order to make a dramatic impression on my students, I smashed it with my heel. What an ignorant move! Do you know that butane lighters explode when smashed? I didn't – and found out the hard way. Lucky for me, no one was injured.

Kids sense through consistent and fair actions if a teacher is in charge of the class. Also avoid idle threats. Think back to when you were a student, and one of your teachers made idle threats; you soon owned that teacher! If you get upset with a child, don't make a foolish statement that you can't back up. Instead, let students know the real consequences of their actions. A case in point was Douglas, also aptly known as "Chicken Man."

Douglas

I'm a strong believer that kids will do exactly what you will allow them to do. In my early years, I inherited some tenth graders from a junior high teacher who was on his way out in more ways than one. He told me he had a student named Douglas who sat in his class and clucked like a chicken. The frustrated teacher claimed he couldn't break him of this annoying habit.

Well, "Chicken Man" was about to crow one last time when he got to my room in September. On one of the first days in my class he tried his chicken routine with me. I bent over so I could look him squarely in the face and said, "You cackle one more time, and I'll pluck your feathers!" He never did it again because I had effectively removed the "communication barrier" between us.

Douglas is now in his forties, and we laugh about that situation every time we see each other. I asked him why he would cackle all the time in junior high school. He admitted it was because the chicken noises bothered the teacher who constantly threatened to punish him, but never did.

Two rules I have always strictly enforced in my classroom: Don't lie to me and never steal from me; anything else we can talk about. I think it's important that your kids know you trust them. When I first started teaching, I had an extremely rowdy group of kids who were almost proud of their untrustworthy reputation. I surprised them one week by proving to them I could bank on their honesty. On a Monday morning in front of several disbelieving pairs of eyes, I tacked a twenty-dollar bill on the bulletin board. I informed them I would take it down Friday afternoon. Friday afternoon arrived, and I removed the untouched bill.

I took a chance by doing that, but it worked. I'm glad it did because in 1971 twenty dollars was a lot of money to a schoolteacher! I specifically remember one of the kids on probation asking me, "Why did you trust us not to steal your money?"

I quietly responded, "You guys are my friends, and you don't steal from your friends."

Without question, I know I gained their respect with that statement. After all these years of teaching, I can't think of a single incident where one of my kids has stolen anything from me.

Another effective rule to enforce is NO TALKING when you are writing on the chalkboard. When you have your back to the class, students will take advantage of a temporary lack of monitoring, and shenanigans occur. If talking is prohibited, *some* of your problems will be eliminated.

A few years ago I had to teach a 19th Century American History course to a class of juvenile delinquents the last period of every day. I didn't even have to turn my back on this group to have the disruptions begin! Students' personal items were stolen or hidden, normally stationary objects became airborne, and other miscellaneous mischief occurred. I quickly realized the only way to keep these students under control was to have them put their book bags and jackets in the front corner of the room. The only items they were allowed to have on their desks were a pencil and one sheet of paper.

For some unknown and merciful reason, they adhered to the rule of no talking while I was writing on the chalkboard. As a result, on particularly stressful days I had a "writing filibuster" on the board. My aide retreated to her desk during many eighth periods trying to keep from laughing out loud as I wrote, and wrote, and wrote. Here's an example of some illustrious notes I slowly and meticulously scribed to create a silent interlude:

The Confederate soldiers, clad in dilapidated, tattered gray uniforms and wearing no shoes, marched into southern Pennsylvania with vengeance on their minds. As the summer sun beat down on their bare heads, they dreamt of home and family while they marched forward with the resolve that they would be victorious. The upcoming conflict with General Meade's blue-clad army, waiting to do battle near the small hamlet of Gettysburg, Pennsylvania, would ultimately decide the fate of the American Civil War.

This writing tactic was a ridiculous coping mechanism, I admit, but it nevertheless helped save my sanity. Occasionally you will be faced with a group of kids who test you beyond what you feel is your limit. Don't let them get to you; figure out something that will work.

And what do you do about individual students you truly dislike? Once again, what you *don't* do is let them know it. In my opinion, you should "bend over backwards" to make sure they never guess your feelings. Over the years I've had a few kids who really got on my nerves, but I made sure not one of them was ever aware of it.

To alleviate this problem, try to get acquainted with the offensive student. I had one young man who thought that he was always right and the whole world was wrong. He honestly drove me crazy, yet I purposely sought opportunities to sit and talk to him. Eventually these chats enabled me to understand the person behind the attitude, making my job much easier. By the time he graduated, I actually enjoyed his company! Of course, this accommodation doesn't always happen, but you must remember these kids have enough problems; on top of everything else, they don't need to know their teacher doesn't particularly like them.

On the flip side of the coin, what do you do when a student doesn't like you and flaunts his dislike in front of you and the rest of the class? While discussing an upcoming videotaping in our classroom, I confided in my students that this event would be very important to me and that I would appreciate their cooperation. One of my new students looked at me and flatly stated, "I'm going to ruin this for you!"

It is human nature to react negatively to that type of "in-your-face" comment, but try to resist that natural temptation and remain calm. Adopting a neutral expression and tone, I asked, "Why do you want to ruin this program?"

He snapped back, "I hate teachers, and I hate school."

I replied, "You don't even know me yet, so how can you hate me?"

"I hate all teachers." His explosive response startled us, and my classroom became uncomfortably quiet.

I paused briefly before responding. Looking directly at him, I mused, "You know, in my lifetime I've only ever been acquainted with one person from China. I liked that boy a great deal, but can I say that I will always like *every* person from China?

Unable to dispute this logic, he said, "No."

"Okay," I continued. "I want to make a deal with you. I want you to judge me solely on being Mr. Riffle. I want to earn your hatred; I don't want to be grouped with anyone else. If you learn to hate me, it's because I'm a jerk, not because of anyone in your past. Is that okay with you?"

He agreed to allow us to develop our own relationship and finished this interesting conversation with one final promise: "When I hate you, I'll tell you!"

I replied, "Fair enough."

Most days when he left my room, I'd stop him and ask, "Well, do you hate me yet?

He'd smile and say, "Not yet, but I'm working on it." He became my friend and learned a valuable lesson in the meantime: Judge people as individuals, not as groups.

Stereotyping is not a fault limited only to students. Obviously, teachers are human and may be predisposed to think disparagingly of students sporting tattoos, rainbow-colored hair, pierced body parts, etc. However, there is another, more subtle form of prejudice that can take place before you ever meet a student.

One habit I have encouraged young teachers *not* to develop is reading permanent records before receiving a new student. No matter how fair-minded you think you are, if you see in black and white that a student was a discipline problem somewhere else, you will also expect that same behavior in your classroom. You may not want to develop such a bias, but that's human nature. I make a point of telling my new students that I don't know anything about their past performances; they will start with a "clean slate" in my room.

June

June came to my class as a tenth grader and immediately caught my attention because of her fragile physique. She was so petite and fine-featured that she reminded me of a China doll. She laughingly revealed in class one day that she wore size zero jeans!

I taught her for three years and found her to be a polite, pleasant, hard worker. At the end of her senior year, when I had to consult her permanent records to finalize some graduation information, I came across some shocking statements from her junior high school teachers. You would have thought this sweet girl was Attila the Hun's granddaughter! This episode just reinforced my belief that all students should be granted a "fresh start" when they come to your class.

Hyperactive children can also be a disruptive force in your classroom. Nowadays, dealing with students who take prescription drugs for ADD/HD is fairly common because the number of students on such medication has skyrocketed in the last twenty years, not just among special education students, but among children in general. Seemingly half the kids in the United States are either presently dependent on a chemical therapy or have been at some time in their lives. Why this alarming trend is occurring is a difficult question to answer. I have a couple theories of my own, but, to be perfectly honest, I don't know if either of them is accurate.

The United States, like many countries, has a very serious drug problem. Has escalating use of illegal drugs by parents caused offspring to be hyperactive? I am aware of specific cases where parents were known drug users and their children are on prescribed medication for hyperactivity. However, I know just as many parents who were not drug users and yet have children on medication to control their behavior.

Maybe it's a new behavior-modification fad to place children on medication every time they give their parents an attitude. When I was young, a father's belt, grounding, or no bike for a week were remedies for poor behavior – not medication! For parents of a child who's just a plain brat, medication provides a socially acceptable excuse for their child's wrongdoing. If Junior tells his mother to take a "flying leap" in front of the next-door neighbor, the parent has an acceptable excuse: *He missed his meds today.* The neighbor understands completely because both of her kids are on meds, too! The situation reminds me of my daughter Rebecca who wanted braces on her teeth in junior high school because all of her friends had them. Instead of carpooling to the orthodontist, parents are now carpooling to the pharmacy. This pill-popping phenomenon may have just become a comfortable, trendy panacea for hyperactivity.

I do not want to discount the importance of these drugs that control hyperactivity and mitigate the effects of attention deficit disorders, nor do I want to imply that these medications are not needed for specific children. I have observed students who were totally out of control when they went off their meds or had their prescriptions changed. These drugs really do a fantastic job for the kids who absolutely need them to correct a genuine problem.

The aforementioned reasons for the upsurge in prescribed drug taking for hyperactivity may not constitute an accurate assessment of the problem. Perhaps a combination of these factors or something completely different is responsible. Regardless of the causes, one irrevocable fact remains: You *will* encounter many medicated children in your classroom.

If you teach special needs students long enough, you will occasionally have an emotionally disturbed child or a brain-injured child in your classroom. Frequently these children will call out during class discussions, annoying both you and their classmates. For these students, one method has produced good results for me over the years; I call it the "beanbag method." The students are given three beanbags (or anything else that is suitable) and a list of rules that is taped to their desks. They are told privately that they must try to cut down on inappropriate statements and questions during class and that these beanbags will help them achieve this goal.

When the class begins, all three bags are put on the front left corner of their desks. If they ask an inappropriate question or make an improper statement anytime during class, I indicate they must move one bag to the right-hand corner. When all three bags have been transferred to the other side of the desk, they may no longer ask questions or make comments. Naturally, they are told that they don't move a bag for an acceptable question or answer. It's somewhat amusing to watch them struggle to be quiet when they are down to their third beanbag.

This technique worked extremely well with one brain-injured student I had a few years ago. He would use up his first two bags during the early part of class and then fidget, trying to control himself from expending his third bag. The amazing outcome was that this boy began to ask appropriate questions in order to save his beanbags. In fact, he would sometimes say, "That question wasn't a beanbag question, was it?"

In dealing with emotionally disturbed or brain-damaged young people, you're going to have good days and bad days, and there isn't much you can do to predict either one. What is effective in keeping them on task in the morning may be totally ineffective two hours later. Therefore, you must be creative, flexible, and have unlimited patience.

Ironically, physically normal students may sometimes resent the students with physical disabilities. This antagonism stems from the fact that the physically challenged students get extra attention from you and the other adults at school. The "normal" children certainly wouldn't want to change places with a wheelchair-bound student, but they do want equal attention, so be prepared for this "attention tension" when working with physically disabled youngsters.

Obviously, there isn't a college course on discipline taught anywhere in the universe that can prepare you for your first teaching assignment. In summary, the only advice I can give you is to post a set of rules that are equitable and then live by them. If a child needs to be disciplined, always make sure the punishment fits the crime. Treat everyone the same way. It is human nature to like certain people more than others, but never show favoritism. One thing that students always respect is fairness.

Being a *real person* to your students is extremely important and can frequently offset discipline problems in the future. Let them see that you are more than just a teacher showing up every day to receive a paycheck. Be remembered as a teacher who was enthusiastic and seemed to truly enjoy being in the company of your students.

I have always believed it is important to connect with your students in non-academic settings: a sporting event, the local mall, their place of employment, or anywhere else you are likely to come in contact with them. Attend anything in which they participate, whether or not it's a school function. One evening I went to a rock concert (if you could call it that) in which one of my kids was playing. It was the poorest excuse for music I've ever heard, but I was there and this "enthusiastic" drummer appreciated my personal interest.

Share your personal life with your students. Tell them about amusing childhood incidents, episodes of teenage indiscretions, and triumphs over fears – real or imagined. Over the years my students have been privy to many strange stories I have related about my own four children at home. When my beloved dog Dotty died in 19 sat in front of my students and cried unashamedly, a natural resp because I perceive my students as part of my family. Don't be afrai. .. reveal your human side – your strengths *and* your weaknesses.

Kids also respond positively to your ability to be flexible and to do spontaneous things. One day Mary walked into class and complained, "I'm tired of the desks facing this way."

Without pause I replied, "Well, maybe it is time for a change. How about if I give you ten minutes to remodel the seating arrangement?" She looked pleased that I had so readily agreed with her and had entrusted her with this responsibility.

"But I might need more like fifteen minutes to make it special," she bargained.

"Okay," I relented. "I'm timing you, and the clock has begun to tick."

Needing no more encouragement, she cleared the kids away from their desks and rearranged the entire room. She was surprisingly creative, pulling the desks out of their ordinary straight rows and pushing them into a clever geometric design. When my second period class arrived, they were amazed and delighted with this transformation from humdrum to "hip." The desks stayed that way for the balance of the school year. Thankfully, the custodian took it all in stride!

Another time one of my students claimed she was bored sitting in every class and wanted to stand. "No problem," I said unhesitatingly. "But we're going to stand on top of our desks." This unexpected answer surprised the class. It must have been a sight to behold – my kids, my aide, and I standing on our desks. The lesson continued without further interruption.

Occasionally, a class majority will plead they don't feel like working that day. Most times I'll give them a "pity party" response or tell them to talk to "Fred" about their troubles. (I have on my desk a deer skull that sports two red golf balls for eyes; he was named Fred many years ago.) But occasionally I'll say, "Okay, class is cancelled for today. Let's just talk." I'll use this time to sit with them and discuss any appropriate subject that comes up. Handled properly, this type of situation earns their respect, and you and your students get to know each other better.

One year I had only three students in my science class. For fun, I challenged these kids to a contest. The premise was simple: All three students had to average eighty percent or higher for the quarter, and, if they did achieve this goal, I promised to buy them pizza for lunch. Since all three of them were good students, I figured that I would probably have to provide pizza four times that year.

Then something totally unexpected happened. Through a series of unforeseen circumstances, six students were suddenly added to my class roster. Some of the new students struggled academically, so I tried tactfully to back out of my agreement. The original three students balked at the very thought of giving up the vision of pizza pies "dancing in their heads!" I was forced to adhere to the first plan.

To my utter surprise, the better students began to tutor their classmates during study halls and, reportedly, even on two occasions at night. All of the students put forth their best effort to maintain good grades so that the entire class could eventually feast on pizza. Missed or incomplete homework was nonexistent in that class. I never saw a group of kids work harder supporting each other in all my years of teaching!

Ultimately, the unchanged plan worked out better than I could ever have imagined, and I was more than happy to buy pizza four times that school year. Truthfully, I cheated once because one child ended up with a seventy-eight point something, so I rounded it up to eighty percent based on effort. Everyone else legitimately scored eighty percent or higher each quarter.

Watching those kids work toward a common goal energized me. Most students do enjoy a challenge. Set a goal – a reasonable and obtainable one – and you will be surprised how hard they will work for you. Do anything to encourage them; do anything to connect with them.

Reaching out to your students can be practiced literally as well as figuratively. My following thoughts about a "touchy" subject might throw your college professors or your administrators into a tailspin. Due to lurid headlines detailing inappropriate conduct, teachers have to be very careful about physical contact with their students. However, a hug doesn't make you a sexual predator. I touch my students all the time; it may be just light contact with a hand or shoulder, or it could entail a full-fledged hug. Somewhere in our overly sensitized society, many people have come to believe that if you touch a child in any manner, you are some sort of pedophile.

A teacher touching a child's arm or shoulder when talking to him or her is a silent sign of caring. Some students never experience any affectionate physical contact at home, and they need that type of human connection to help them develop a healthy amount of self-esteem. I've had certain kids hug me every day when they came to my class because I was the only outlet for affection in their lives.

One of my boys, standing 6'6" and weighing 235 pounds, was very distraught one day over the death of a relative. I wrapped my arms around him gently and told him how sorry I was, and I could tell immediately by his reaction that someone holding him was not a circumstance to which he was accustomed.

A couple of months later, I broached this subject with him, and he admitted he hadn't been hugged since he was a small child. That's quite a startling statement coming from a nineteen-year-old boy. It's hard to imagine growing up all those years and never having anyone hold you just because he or she cares. Such emotional deprivation in a young person's life is often detrimental to the development of interpersonal relationships.

The "hugging" story I've always enjoyed relating concerns two sisters, Connie and Christine. Christine's older sister, Connie, graduated the year before Christine came to tenth grade. Over the Christmas holiday, I saw Connie at the mall, and, during the course of the conversation, I asked her how Christine was enjoying tenth grade. Connie laughed and said, "Christine says you're a good teacher, but an even better hugger." I took that as a major compliment, not as an endorsement for being a pedophile!

My students touch me all the time in totally appropriate ways. Once – out of curiosity – I kept track of the number of kids who touched me throughout the course of a school day. Twenty-three students initiated physical contact with me in some manner. I deemed it as nothing more than letting another human being know that they care.

I had an Asian student who was learning-disabled, had a speech impediment, and spoke English as a second language. Frequently, it was very difficult to understand much of what he was saying in class. The day before I left for the American Teacher Awards presentation in California, my students threw a going-away party. As this young man was ready to leave for the day, he walked up to me, put his hand on my shoulder, and very clearly said, "I will miss you." His kindness and sincerity touched me deeply. Whenever I'm having a bad day and my emotional batteries are drained, I reflect on this type of experience to get me jump-started again.

Much like their teachers, students sometimes need help generating interest and enthusiasm for learning. Your teaching style and techniques can play a vital role in this endeavor. What teaching styles will you use in your classroom? You may be tempted to mimic a former teacher you admired, but the bottom line is that you must be yourself. Just as we know students have different learning styles, educators have different teaching styles, and one is not superior to the other. What is right for you is not always suitable for another teacher.

In all of my classes, I strive to have a relaxed atmosphere in which the students feel comfortable learning and at ease expressing their own ideas and opinions. I use humor and a large number of anecdotes in my daily lessons. This approach, which works for me, wouldn't necessarily work for someone else. Teaching styles are a lot like hitting a baseball: There are certain basic fundamentals you must use, but then you have to develop your own technique.

Underlying any style or technique must be your belief that all students, no matter how severe their disabilities, can learn. Your responsibility as an educator is to make sure that happens. Be flexible and creative in your approach to the material that must be taught. Even in a small class of fifteen students, different learning styles are evident, so adapting the right method to each learning situation is critical. I have worked with young people whose IQ's ranged from forty up to and including the gifted range. Obviously, life skills youngsters can't match the gifted child in the amount of material retained or the time required to obtain that material, but they *can* learn.

Bobby

During my first year of teaching, I had a young boy named Bobby who had a full-scale IQ of 48 and couldn't read or write anything other than his first name. After struggling for weeks to help him learn a few simple words, I came up with the idea of food as a motivator. I labeled index cards with his sight-reading words, bought a pack of penny candy, and kept my fingers crossed that I might find success with my new technique.

I gave him a single piece of candy to eat and then put a piece of candy on each card. I told him he could have the candy if he knew the word. The results were dramatic; dozens of new words were added to his sight vocabulary. Eventually, he recognized so many words that he was allotted a reward only for every five words he correctly identified. I joked with my co-workers that there was good news and bad news: Bobby could read now, but he put on an extra seventy-five pounds! I finally switched from candy to plastic army figures, and two years later he was successfully reading on a first-grade level.

Believing that all students can learn is a positive concept that can unfortunately become a negative one if taken to an extreme level. Inclusion seems to be the key word when working with learning support students in the Twenty-first Century. The possibility of one of my better academic kids taking a mainstream academic course many years ago was "zero to none." Now, through new legislation, these students are eligible to take basically any course they desire. Honestly, I feel the pendulum has swung too far to the other side as it frequently does in the wake of contentious court cases.

If a child has the ability to succeed in mainstream academic courses, I'm all for the placement. The problem is that students who lack academic ability are being placed in college preparatory classes. Educators are then given the unrealistic job of making sure these children experience achievement. There are only two possible routes to "success": The regular education teacher just gives out a free grade, or the special education teacher does all of the work.

My viewpoint may be controversial, but it's also based on years of observation. I would love to have all of my students attend Harvard or Yale, but that's not going to happen. This situation is also unfair to the regular education teacher and the other students. Some professionals and parents have the notion that all children are college material, and all that you have to do is work hard enough with them to achieve that academic level. This type of thinking can be very harmful to a child.

I clearly remember such a case I encountered more than thirty-five years ago involving a nine-year-old little girl who came from a family of professional people and was mentally retarded. The day her school administered standardized testing, her parents told her she would do better than her classmates and make her family proud. She was so upset that as she sat in front of me, she lost bladder control. I felt very bad for this child because even after I talked to the parents, relentless pressure for unattainable academic achievement continued. Sadly, the parents were more concerned about their own egos than about the child's well-being.

Many learning support students do extend their formal education past high school. When they discuss their future education plans with you, therefore, you must consider all students individually and ask them why they want to continue their education. This obligation holds true for regular education students as well. Today so many kids want to go to college because they feel that in our society everyone is *expected* to go to college. The conversations I've held with several students usually followed the same format:

"What are you going to do following graduation?"

" Go to college."

"What will be your major?"

"I don't know."

"Then why go until you have a goal in mind?"

"Everyone's supposed to go to college."

One of the most difficult challenges for any special education teacher is dealing with the academic expectations of the parents and students. To recommend or to not recommend college is an extremely tough call for any teacher to make. My own academic orientation was a prime example of this problem. There wasn't a single teacher I ever had in high school who thought I would be capable of graduating from college. In fact, as I related in Chapter 1, my college advisor told me to quit school and join the army.

Because of my own experience, my advice is to allow these students to give college a try; they will find out soon enough if college is feasible for them. This reasoning always seemed logical to me and worked for years – until, that is, Frank asked me if I thought he should go to college.

Frank

Frank was a super-nice kid whom we all enjoyed having in class. However, he stubbornly clung to the notion that if you didn't graduate from college, you would be a failure as an adult. He had a severe learning disability but kept insisting he had to go to college. I counseled him that college is just an opportunity for additional education – no more, no less. I encouraged him to give it his best shot. I also tried to reassure him that if it didn't work out, he would find his niche somewhere else.

His reply worried me.

"Mr. Riffle, I must make it; what would happen to me if I don't?

I told him again, "Just do your best and see what happens, but don't make college a life-or-death situation."

I advised him to enroll at a community college, a successful alternative for many learning support kids. Frequently, the classes are smaller, and the staff works closely with the students. But Frank didn't want to hear anything about that. His best friend was going to a four-year school, and he was determined to do the same.

During the second semester of his freshman year, I received a frantic phone call from his mother. Frank had tried to kill himself. Although he wasn't successful, he was very seriously injured. This fine young man who had so much to live for almost died because he put so much emphasis on a college education.

Fortunately, Act 101 has since been instituted to assist learning support students in college. This program supplies tutors and other support systems to help these students succeed. Since the opportunities for assistance vary greatly from one college to another, students and their parents should scrutinize the Act 101 program at each college very carefully before enrollment.

Half the battle is won when you've developed varied and interesting methods that reflect your conviction that all students can learn. However, the most critical turning point involves convincing the students themselves that they can learn. Positive reinforcement is essential within your classroom: always encourage, never discourage.

To ensure this attitude of acceptance takes root, there is another classroom rule that I strictly enforce from the very first day of every school year: *No one ever makes fun of anyone's wrong answer.* Students must understand that they will never be ridiculed by their classmates for an incorrect response. I tell them that everyone makes mistakes because that's just part of life. Be the role model and make sure that you – the classroom teacher – don't give verbal cues, gestures, or expressions that disparage a child.

Sometimes you will receive an answer that is "light years" away from the correct response to a question. Refrain from saying or doing anything that could be negatively construed by the student. Instead, you might want to say something like "I didn't phrase my question clearly enough, so let me put it another way." This response takes the pressure off the child in a very simple and gentle way.

Make question and answer sessions with your students upbeat and fun. A technique that you might occasionally want to try is paying for correct answers to certain questions. Announce beforehand that they are about to hear a nickel, dime, or quarter question; only one guess is allowed. The kids love this little incentive and generally follow the lesson more attentively. It's surprising how often they will return the coins after class since they aren't as concerned about winning the money as they are about showing you they know the answer.

I hesitate employing team-type games when reviewing material for two reasons. Invariably, one or two kids dominate the contest. The interest level of the other, less-involved participants wanes rather quickly, defeating the whole purpose of the activity. Also, if a team loses as the result of one child making a mistake, that student may be very reluctant to participate the next time the same activity is proposed.

There are always children in your classes so withdrawn they will not interact with you during a question-and-answer exercise. For the teacher to get the quiet ones involved is quite a challenge. Although there is no simple solution that is successful every time, the "easy-question technique" has often worked for me. Find a fact or two that you are sure they will know, and then ask them questions dealing with that information. After they consistently answer these questions correctly, their confidence levels increase, and, before long, these quieter students will be interacting with their classmates.

I once had a young woman whose IQ was in the mid forties. Every time I reviewed for a test, I developed a set of true and false questions. I always made sure to ask her a question that was true. Invariably, she answered it correctly, and no one ever seemed to notice our routine. This procedure was followed for three years, and she always felt like an integral part of the group during each chapter review.

True or False: *Sticks and stones can break my bones, but words can never hurt me.* The answer in this case is definitely *false,* and the two groups of people who should never abuse a child with words are parents and teachers. We've all done it, whether intentionally or unintentionally, out of pure frustration. I've committed this error with my own kids at home and with students in my classroom. Sometimes you don't even realize that you've hurt them, but if you do, apologizing is an excellent way to rectify the situation. I've stood in front of my class on more than one occasion and apologized to a student because I was wrong. It's amazing how much respect you will gain by admitting publicly that you were out of line. As I've mentioned before, being a real person to your students is paramount.

Matthew

When my son Matthew was in eighth grade, I overheard a conversation he had with his science teacher on the last day of the marking period. She informed him that he had 79% for the quarter, and she was going to go home and think about whether he was a nice kid or not. She further explained that if he *had* been a nice kid, she would give him the extra percentage point. Matt told her that one extra point would put him on the honor roll.

When the report cards came out, Matt had 79%, not the 80% she had teasingly suggested he might receive. I had a very upset young man in my house that night because he maintained that he had always been nice to her and had never given her any problems in class.

It's very difficult as a parent to explain that situation. If she wasn't going to give him the extra point, that was her prerogative as a teacher. However, she shouldn't have told him his grade was based on his being a nice kid. I'm sure she never gave it another thought, but Matthew certainly did. We must always be careful when speaking to students because, believe it or not, they are sometimes listening very carefully to us.

Phil

One of our teachers came within inches of being punched by one of my boys. Phil, a varsity athlete who was very strong and quick-tempered, was mainstreamed for math during his senior year. On several occasions he reported his teacher had repeatedly ridiculed him in class. I kept telling Phil that maybe the teacher was only kidding him and cautioned him to remain calm. I reminded him that he needed that class for graduation and suggested that if anything demeaning happened in the future, he should come directly to my classroom.

Only a few days later, Phil stormed into my classroom so furious that I thought he was going to pop a blood vessel! He started ranting and raving about this "stupid" teacher. Since one of my classroom rules forbids students from making derogatory statements about other teachers, I took him to an empty classroom across the hall to calm him so I could find out what had happened.

Phil told me he had simply asked the teacher a question, and the teacher had responded, "You're even dumber than I thought you were!" Fortunately, Phil was able to control himself and leave the room before he went for that man's throat. The teacher was fully aware that Phil was a learning support student. I was able to verify Phil's story later that day and was told it had happened just as he had reported.

This type of situation puts a teacher in an awkward position because you don't want to go up against a colleague, and yet you must protect the integrity of your kids. Obviously, no teacher in any class should ever call a child dumb, but, if you say the wrong thing, the majority of the faculty may ostracize you and your students. I discussed this incident with my principal, who wanted to confront the teacher. I asked him to refrain, however, because there were only a few days left in the quarter, and we could move Phil to another class in the new quarter. This boy had no chance to experience success by remaining in a setting that would destroy his fragile self-esteem. Helping a child develop self-confidence – not destroying it – is critical to the learning process.

Sara

In the mid-1990s, a young woman named Sara came to registration with a terrible fear of schools. When she arrived, she sat silently with tears coursing down her face. As the adults discussed her proposed education plan, Sara remained mute. Fortunately for Sara, our emotional support teacher came into her life. She gently worked with Sara and eased her into a comfortable daily routine at our school.

At the beginning of the term, Sara's schedule consisted of English and math; following second period, she was allowed to go home. This schedule was in place until November when it was increased to half a day. By March she was coming to school full-time. Eventually Sara graduated from high school and found employment in the state park system.

We have had a great deal of success working with young people suffering from school phobia. Our initial goal is to have them attend long enough to take one learning support class. The incoming students are interviewed in order to find out which course would be of interest to them. The course selection really isn't the primary concern; of paramount importance is getting these children into a school setting devoid of academic pressure. Eventually, the students begin to feel at ease and – within a relatively short time – attend school on a half-day, if not a full-day, basis.

School phobia may seem implausible to some adults, but it is more common among children than most people realize. Perception is a favorite word of mine in dealing with students. Whether a problem is real or not is irrelevant; if a person perceives it as real, then it *is* real to him or her. Case in point: Santa Claus!

The students who lack self-confidence will often inadvertently reveal themselves by what they say or do. Simple key phrases can alert you to the problem: *This is too hard; I can't learn this stuff; I'm not smart enough to learn this.* Such remarks frequently indicate doubts about their own abilities. Sometimes you have to be an "emotional cheerleader" for your students. This means you have to find positive ways to build their self-confidence.

Kim

One memorable teaching incident confirmed for me the undeniable link between self-confidence and learning. In the late Seventies I had a tall young woman named Kim in my tenth-grade English class. Every Friday I gave a twenty-question, matching vocabulary test. Kim didn't have a single word correct on the first two tests, and I wanted to know why. She told me she was too dumb to take those tests. After I firmly told her she was never to call herself dumb again, she promised to study for the following week's test.

That Friday I asked her if she had studied for the vocabulary test. She nodded, then not too convincingly replied, "A little." I arranged for her to take the matching test with a pencil – a zero again. I erased her answers, wrote in the correct answers, and put 100% at the top of her paper. She almost fell over when she saw her score. Her grades improved week after week until she actually earned a 100% on her own. By the time she graduated, Kim was one of my top vocabulary students!

Over the years Kim has stayed in contact with me. One day I decided to divulge the truth about her first few vocabulary tests. When I told her, she started to cry, hugged me, and said, "I always did love you." I explained to her that I had simply instilled her with confidence in her ability to learn. She is now in her forties and has assured me that the confidence I gave her has helped immensely in her adult life.

Someone once asked what I would have done if that ruse hadn't been successful. I really didn't know what to answer, except that I would have tried something else until I found a technique that worked. You will frequently have students with very low self-esteem, and you must use any means possible to develop a positive self-image so they can start believing in themselves.

Now comes the time to have faith in yourself. You are no longer a student teacher; you're on your own and about to embark on the most amazing journey of your life. Becoming a teacher endows you with an awesome responsibility: You are entrusted with the obligation to nurture and help mold young people's lives. Your goal, and the goal of teachers everywhere, is to give your students the best education possible. Don't settle for being a good teacher; be a great teacher! The most important advice is really very simple: Teach with your heart; your subject matter will take care of itself.

Good Luck!

GUIDELINES TO HELP YOU BECOME
A SUCCESSFUL SPECIAL EDUCATION TEACHER

1. Teach with your heart; your subject matter will take care of itself.

2. Make a positive difference with children.

3. Trust and respect are earned; they are not guaranteed because you're a teacher.

4. All children can learn; if one method doesn't work, try something else.

5. Never make idle threats.

6. Be a real person to your students; let them know you truly LOVE them and care about them.

7. Listen more and talk less.

8. Be flexible and creative in your approach to education.

9. Building confidence in a child is critical to the learning process.

10. Positive reinforcement in your classroom is essential; always encourage, never discourage.

11. Patience is a true virtue for special education teachers. Never give up on a student; you may be all they have.

12. All students get a fresh start when they first come to your room.

13. You are a role model for your students. Strive for excellence because you never know where your influence starts and stops.

CHAPTER 4

"Knowledge is power, but enthusiasm pulls the switch."

... Ivern Ball

— Pearl Harbor was attacked by Japan on December 7, 1941.

— President Abraham Lincoln issued the Emancipation Proclamation on January 1, 1863.

— The Battle of Antietam was the bloodiest day in American history.

— The Law of Demand states that consumers will buy more of a product as the price goes down.

— The body temperature of warm-blooded animals remains constant.

— Nouns name a person, place or thing.

— The hypotenuse is the side of a right triangle opposite the right angle...

One hundred and eighty days; such a short season for teachers to transplant a vast array of facts, theories, and concepts into the fertile young minds entrusted to them. Fire drills, standardized testing, health checks, school pictures, assemblies and other chronic interruptions further erode even *that* precious block of time. And, barring a natural disaster or a terrorist attack, what could be more traumatic nowadays than the dire announcement over the intercom system that the computers are down?

However, it's not just the amount of time spent teaching that is important; equally significant is the time invested in setting the stage for learning to take place – the physical environment, lesson plans, and motivational techniques. These three powerful factors contribute immensely to the quantity *and* the quality of learning that occurs in a classroom. The good news is that these educational domains are almost totally controlled by you – the teacher – and are virtually resistant to outside interference. Sabotage takes place only if these components are not fortified with contagious enthusiasm, a good sense of humor, and a genuine caring attitude.

If teachers are not truly excited about their subject matter, students cannot reasonably be expected to become eager learners. This premise was verified for me one day while teaching a botany unit in biology class. A student, *Homo sapiens egobusterus,* bluntly informed me that my lectures on plants were not as stimulating as the ones on animals. Admittedly, I never enjoyed teaching botany, but I didn't realize my lack of passion for plants was so obvious to my students. Later, just out of curiosity, I pulled out my grade book to compare their overall progress in both units. Sure enough, I had the visual proof that the grades were lower in the botany unit. The lack of achievement wasn't entirely their fault; these students were sitting in front of an uninspired teacher!

The teacher is indisputably the most important element in any educational setting, but classroom presentation also greatly affects the learning climate. Most chefs would agree that shrimp is the chief ingredient in a shrimp salad, but if the bed of greens is brown and wilted, this delicacy is not very appetizing. Similarly, the classroom environment must be welcoming, projecting an inviting atmosphere that encourages the acquisition of knowledge. Gone are the days when special education classes are relegated to some dingy, out-of-the way room.

Fortunately, a degree in interior decorating is not necessary to transform a *blah* room into an *ah* room. Start with the basics. No matter what subject or grade is being taught, a plain room can be revitalized with colorful posters and decorated bulletin boards. Education stores and catalogues offer a wide variety of materials from which to choose.

Ideas from these sources may also provide the imaginative spark needed to tailor the room to your own needs.

After a bright, cheerful atmosphere has been established, go one step further: Personalize your room. Display memorabilia and photographs that reveal your own interests, hobbies, and other leisure-time activities. Family portraits, fishing and hunting pictures, as well as a photo gallery devoted to former students adorn various areas of my room. While creating a more comfortable and homier atmosphere, such visual arrangements also serve as springboards for countless student-initiated conversations, fostering better rapport overall with students. Think of these exhibits as miniature billboards that advertise you as a *real human being*!

Of course, classroom décor needs more input than just the teacher's. As the school year progresses, student artwork and projects should be conspicuously incorporated into the surroundings. One fun project is painting the replaceable ceiling tiles in your room. These small panels are inexpensive and can be purchased at any hardware store. At the end of the year, these *highly* regarded works of art can be retained or returned to their creators. Students take great pride in having their work showcased. Displays also convey to them that the teacher appreciates their efforts and admires their talents.

To promote creative ability, I reserve a certain shelf in my room just for the framed drawings of extremely artistic students. Since this exhibit is more permanent, garnering a spot on this "shelf of fame" signifies a special honor. A sophomore named Harry seemed especially drawn to this side of the room and often gazed at the miniature gallery. One day he tentatively asked me what prerequisites must be met to have artwork selected for *the shelf*. I kindly informed him that this space was reserved for seniors and former students only. Seeing his crestfallen expression, I instantly amended that statement and allowed for the *rare* possibility of discovering exceptional underclassman talent. A conspiratorial wink followed my admission. Like a thief taking advantage of an open window, Harry trespassed onto forbidden territory presenting me one week later with a finely detailed pencil sketch of a special inhabitant of our classroom. This endeavor justly earned Harry the proud distinction of being the first underclassman to have his work adorn *the shelf.*

Occasionally, a more reticent artist surfaces. I noticed that whenever Eric put his name on an assignment, a tiny, delicate rose – sometimes executed in vivid colors – invariably followed his signature. I often complimented his flowery John Hancock. He seemed extremely pleased, yet surprised, when I requested one of his drawings for the room. This newly commissioned artist seemed puzzled and asked me *what* I wanted him to draw. I told him I didn't think that should be such a *thorny* issue! Thinking he had missed my poor attempt at humor, I didn't know what to expect when he handed me a piece of paper a few days later. However, I wasn't disappointed. As if plucked right from the garden, Eric's rose still blooms on *the shelf.*

Other times you will discover a student's ability purely by chance. One year my senior students were working on a group project for economics. Part of the assignment required them to create an appropriate logo for an imaginary company. While most kids used the computer art programs, Paul, I noticed, was working meticulously on his group's logo at his desk. I remember thinking that no matter how poor his art ability, I would judge him solely on his effort. When he presented me with the hand-drawn logo, I was amazed by his beautiful rendition of a unicorn. When I recovered my voice, I said, "Paul, you never told me you were an artist." His innocent reply was, "Well, you never asked me!"

At this point, it's quite possible to bring the room to life – or more accurately – to bring life to the room. In addition to plants, classroom pets can add another interesting dimension to the environment. Critters such as snakes, turtles, lizards, ferrets, rabbits, hamsters, gerbils, guinea pigs, and mice fascinate children of any age. In our class the star pupil is a green parakeet named Pauper Boy. This sociable little guy has flown right into all of our hearts and has become a regular member of the class.

When I'm working in my classroom on weekends, Pauper Boy is uncharacteristically quiet and takes only a few lofty laps around the room. However, as soon as the kids arrive on Monday morning, he perks up and clings to his door, begging to escape the confines of his cage so he can zoom into the day's activities. To the delight of the students, his flight plans usually include trips to their desks, the computers, and even to the podium when I am lecturing. Sometimes he forsakes all of us, preferring to land on *the shelf* and vainly preen in front of his portrait contributed by Harry!

Pauper Boy shares both the limelight and his counter space with two angelfish housed in a ten-gallon aquarium. Across the room on a low filing cabinet, a small goldfish bowl nestles among some fossil rocks. Coincidentally, this small body of water also doubles as a birdbath. (And, coincidence or not, the parakeet always takes his cleansing plunges on a Friday!)

Although properly maintaining living creatures in the room may require a little bit of extra time and money, ample repayment flows back into the till in other subtle ways. One of my wheelchair-bound girls had a special attachment to our goldfish that she aptly named Pigfish. She took it upon herself to feed him every morning as soon as she entered the room. When she wheeled over to his bowl, the fish raced to the surface to wait for breakfast. Even on days when she was upset, Pigfish's self-appointed guardian never forgot her duty to care for him. Watching him swim slowly in lazy, mesmerizing circles actually seemed to relax her and help her regain the ability to focus on tasks. Upon her graduation, she not only received a well-earned diploma, but also a gift of "gold" – Pigfish!

In addition to providing therapeutic benefits, our pets are also impressed into service as educational props. What could be handier than having a parakeet in residence to demonstrate different types of feathers and their functions? Sometimes, Pauper Boy actually cooperates and molts in a timely fashion so the kids have a chance to more closely examine these lightweight specimens! *Conditioned responses* are clearly observable and identifiable by the students as they watch the angelfish surface to receive food when the aquarium hood creaks open or listen to the parakeet screech to get out when he hears the distinctive rattle of the keys that lock the classroom door before he is given his freedom. Economics students grasp that there is a huge market for new products for pets, and these budding entrepreneurs are urged to use their ingenuity to develop a marketable item as one of their projects. Truly, the ongoing list of possibilities for pet involvement in education is limited only by the boundaries of the teacher's imagination.

Although students can be led into a pleasant classroom environment, their surroundings don't automatically guarantee they will demonstrate a desire to learn. As any teacher will freely admit, motivating all students is not a simple task. Learning-disabled students often perceive the educational process as a painful procedure they have to endure for twelve or more years before they can get on with the rest of their lives! This defeatist attitude, as well as an ever-increasing array of outside distractions that vie for their attention, present formidable obstacles for today's educators.

Creating stimulating lesson plans can be an especially daunting challenge for the rookie teacher. Frequently overwhelmed by meetings, clerical work, and responsibilities not even remotely associated with subject matter, the first-year teacher has a tendency to rely solely on textbooks and standardized, company-prepared material to muddle through the initial school term. Fortunately, many school districts now offer a one or two-year mentoring program to assist new staff members. Veteran teachers are also an invaluable resource for advice and new ideas. I wish I had been so lucky at the beginning of my career; I was given a classroom with thirty students and was left alone to fend for myself.

One important resource I eventually started to utilize was the local community. Business people, veterans, and members of service organizations have willingly donated their time to bring firsthand information and expertise to my students. Finding people who can enrich your lessons can be simplified by creating a questionnaire for each student's family to complete. This form will secure such basic information as name, address, phone, and occupation. More specific questions should be included that pertain to a military career, hobbies, travel destinations, unusual life experiences, etc. If every teacher comprises a list and then shares it with co-workers, the resource list will be quite extensive. Another possible method to reach an even wider population is to include such a survey in a district-wide newsletter. Using modern technology, the responses can be returned via e-mail.

Learning World War II history seems like a waste of time to many students today, evoking such discouraging comments as *Why do we need to learn about stuff that happened sixty years ago? My parents weren't even born then!* However, this apathetic attitude undergoes a heartening transformation as students pay close attention to local veterans who appear in my Twentieth Century History course for one day every year to relate their wartime experiences. Textbooks are a necessity for dates, names, and facts, but these former soldiers, who served their country in both the European and Pacific Theaters, put a face to the war and bring history to life.

Ron was a Pearl Harbor veteran who fought with the Marines throughout the Pacific Campaign. In the middle of recounting his war experiences, he paused and said, "You know, you could easily tell the difference between decaying Jap bodies and American bodies. They smelled so different; it must have been their diets." He never seemed to notice the collective startled reaction of his young audience. With widened eyes and mouths agape, they stared at each other in disbelief; they had never thought about the absolute horror of real war.

Another Pearl Harbor survivor, Joe, was describing his recollection of the battle when a student asked him if he had ever seen a Japanese pilot up close. Joe said, "Well, yes and no. One Jap plane crashed near us, and the pilot burned up in his cockpit. When the fire was out, my buddy pulled the pilot's thigh bone out of the wreckage, cleaned it off with his pocketknife, and kept it as a souvenir!"

The following day history books were set aside. The entire period was devoted to discussing the veterans' presentations and the students' reactions to some of the grim wartime revelations. One girl remarked that she found it upsetting that these men had exhibited such a matter-of-fact attitude about killing other people. I tried to explain to her that these former soldiers were not trying to shock the class; they were simply relating what life was like for them as teenagers thrust into war where every day, as front-line soldiers, they woke up knowing somewhere there were other men whose sole purpose was to kill them – a reality not documented in their textbooks.

The unforgettable manner in which another veteran materialized in my classroom belongs in *Ripley's Believe It or Not!* Introducing a lesson highlighting General James Doolittle's Raid on Japan to my 20th Century History class, I said, "I'm going to tell you about an historical event that you've probably never heard of called Doolittle's Raid on Japan."

Those words were barely out of my mouth when one boy fired his hand into the air and declared, "I know about that attack."

I said, "Great, Chris, how did you learn about it? Did you see it on the History Channel?"

Matter-of-factly, Chris stated, "No, my grandfather was one of the pilots."

"Your grandfather flew in Doolittle's raid?" I incredulously queried. "Is he still alive?"

Chris said, "Sure, he lives in California with my grandmother."

His casual reply was in stark contrast to my own mounting excitement following this startling disclosure. *What were the chances that the grandson of one of Doolittle's fliers was sitting right in front of me!* Thrilled by this unexpected discovery, I had Chris call his mother immediately to obtain the grandfather's phone number. Minutes later – right there in class – I had the distinct privilege of speaking to one of the brave men who flew a B-25 bomber, normally a land-based plane, from the deck of the aircraft carrier U.S.S. Hornet in the surprise attack on Japan on April 18, 1942. While his grandfather was graciously agreeing to videotape an interview based on questions from the class, Chris just sat there staring at me wondering what all the fuss was about!

Inspired by such encounters with veterans, I have developed a World War II project entitled *Battlefield Experience* for my learning support Twentieth Century American History course. Three class periods, preferably on consecutive days, are devoted to simulating combat and other events that are part of a soldier's life. In setting up this project, I simply inform the students that for three days they must pretend they are American soldiers in France in 1944. From this point on they are not bombarded with a lot of forgettable facts, but rather are immersed in a memorable and emotional learning experience – one that produces incredible creative writing and enthusiastic participation by almost every student.

Day One- The students are told they are going to be involved in a major battle the next day and that some of them will not be coming back. Sweeping them immediately into the past, I announce that their commanding general is about to speak to them. The lights are turned off, and they view the famous "flag speech" from the movie *Patton,* starring George C. Scott as the legendary commander.

Following that fiery speech, the students are required to confront their own mortality and take part in a traditional ritual most combat soldiers engage in before facing the enemy: writing good-bye letters to their families. The students are warned that this may be the very last time they will ever communicate with their loved ones as these letters will be mailed home if they are killed.

The letters that are written during the first phase of this project demonstrate how seriously the students approach this thought-provoking task. One foster child penned this message to his foster parents:

Tomorrow I am going to be in my first battle. I know what I'm doing is right and for my country, but I'm really scared and so are lots of my buddies.

Thanks for taking me in and letting me live in your house. I know it has only been three months that I've lived with you, but it has meant a lot to me. You have made me feel like I am your real son. You do so much for me to take care of me, and I really appreciated all of your efforts to do this, but I never told you before. Now is the time I feel I must write this because I may not have the chance to do so again.

Andy, I miss playing basketball with you; you really taught me a lot about the sport. I hope you play with the Bulls some day.

Melinda, I know I'm not there to help you learn to ride your bike but please keep practicing. Give Tinker and Gizzy a pat on the head for me.

I will always love all of you.

The young person who composed the next letter came from a very tragic home situation: One parent had committed suicide, and the remaining parent was physically abusive. This letter was written to the grandparents who had taken custody of the boy and raised him in a more stable environment.

I don't know how to explain clearly what I am going to tell you next. Tomorrow I'm going into battle and may not come back. Words themselves cannot describe how scared I am. You have always said that I can be anything I wanted to be as long as I put my heart and soul into it, but I don't think that will work out tomorrow. You all have been there for me; you would have moved mountains for me and I sincerely appreciate it. Your never-ending love protected me like a fortress.

I am going to miss you all more than you will ever know. I feel as though I am already dead 'cause my heart is killing me. I will always be in your hearts as you have always been in mine.

The young woman who wrote the following letter (and to whom this book is dedicated) died three years later. While writing this chapter, I realized this was, in fact, a genuine good-bye letter. I copied the letter and gave the original version to the family, who assured me they would always cherish this gift as if their daughter had revisited them to deliver one final message.

I'm going into battle tomorrow, and I'm writing because I might not make it out alive. Please, Mom and Dad, tell Marcy and Michael that I love them and will miss them very much.

Mom, I'm sitting in a shed, and it's very cold and wet. I'm thinking about my whole life and how it may be taken away from me tomorrow. I'm very sad and upset. General Patton spoke to us, and I'm not sure what I'm supposed to do tomorrow.

I have to carry a gun, and I don't like the idea of shooting someone. We have started to dig graves, and I don't want to end up in one of these graves. I don't want to have to bury my friends either.

I'm sitting here remembering all the great times we had when we went camping at Knoebels.

I remember growing up and how you made my birthday and Christmas so special each year. Mom, I really could eat a bowl of your delicious goulash right now!

I will always love you very much. Please take care of each other.

As stated, this exercise has quite an emotional impact on students. While they are writing these messages, the room is unnaturally quiet. Some kids silently shed tears as they write what is in their hearts. They are always told not to worry about grammar or spelling at this point – just write. I encourage them to share these letters with their parents. Since parents and teenagers are frequently at odds, these "final messages" can possibly improve strained relationships. The following excerpt, for instance, exposed some raw emotional wounds in the life of one student:

I devoted my whole life into trying to make you happy, but I feel that my best wasn't good enough. I joined the army to be a man like Dad always tried to beat into my head. I served my country with love and loyalty, but only to feel I failed you again. All those times I told you to leave me alone, I actually wanted your attention.

This letter revealed painful and unresolved thoughts festering in this young person's mind. The information was relayed to our school psychologist, who, in turn, arranged counseling services for the family.

Day Two- This phase is called The Battle Day. When the students come into the room, the shades are drawn and the lights are turned off. They are told to put their heads down, listen to a tape that simulates the din of battle, and imagine they are actually engaged in fighting the enemy.

The students are also forewarned that sometime during the tape I might approach their desks and cover them with something soft. These particular individuals are instructed to remain motionless when I turn the lights back on. The tape lasts approximately twenty minutes and is enhanced by a strobe light flashing relentlessly as the harsh sounds of combat fill the room.

While the deafening sound effects engulf everyone, red or white sheets are placed over certain students. When the tape ends, the students not covered are told to sit up as the draped bodies remain motionless. The people covered in red represent the wounded, and the people covered in white symbolize the dead. As the "survivors" quietly survey their surroundings, I somberly remind them that this is what war is like: "The friends with whom you ate dinner the night before are now dead. The fact is that people killed in battle are blown to bits; it isn't like someone who dies from a heart attack. There is blood and gore everywhere."

The students are shown another scene from *Patton* depicting the aftermath of a battle. Their creative writing assignment for Day Two is to describe the mental and physical sensations they experienced during the fighting. The following essays illustrate the astounding insight these students displayed while explaining their feelings.

The same day of the battle, it's over now kind of. We fought a long and vicious battle for hours on end with the sound of murder in my ears, the blood of the enemy on my hands, dried to my skin. As I look around all I see are bodies, not faces or colors, just bodies, which brings me to the conclusion that no one won the battle. We were all losers, but that's really what we came here to do is die. But the battle in my mind has just begun!

Ed

Everything was happening too fast to really take in. I heard yelling, bombs, machine guns, and airplanes. It was so fast that you didn't know what was happening around you, so you didn't know what to think but fear. The thought of seeing your best friends lying there dead and wounded was more than I could take. I wanted to help them but I was powerless; it was horrible. How will the families of my dead friends react to losing their sons?

The voices in the distance were confusing, but the screams and the yelling hit me like a ton of bricks. People died for their country and served a purpose, but it was more important to live and fight on. More than a handful dropped dead around me while the guns and tanks roared.

The shot that hit me, hit me hard, and I knew that I was dying, so I just sat down and gave up while the others around me fought and killed.

The thing that gets me was that at that point I was unable to fight, so I knew I was expendable. No one stopped to help me, and no one cared but me. And then it happened. Like a flash I was hit again!
Charles

I saw a lot of people die. There was no reason for all of these people to die. There were dead and wounded lying everywhere. The guns kept firing, and there was a terrible odor from the guns and the dead bodies. Every step you took, you walked over a dead body and you couldn't get the sound of the wounded out of your mind.

Jim

The battle was very long with bloody battlefields and loud sounds of the never-ending gunshots as well as the sounds of screams and cries for home and families, the sounds of the guns being fired and hearing them pierce the bodies of humans and hearing their dead lifeless corpses hit the ground. There are many dead soldiers lying on the ground in puddles of blood that look like a dark red wine and many injured men crying for help or claiming to be in pain and wanting to die. In the background of all this chaos are the sounds of tanks and landmines going off and the sight of legs, arms, and even heads flying towards the ground. The guns firing that never stops is deafening. The guilt that I feel right now for killing these men is hard even for me to describe. I feel like I have to kill myself to repent for what I have done even though it really won't make up for it. The sounds of the guns and the screams that are heard are still going, and I don't think that they will ever stop.

Holly

Day Three- The third and final stage of *Battlefield Experience* concerns the aftermath of the battle. The students are informed that the United States government has notified the families of killed, wounded, or missing-in-action soldiers with telegrams that frequently were delivered by high school kids on bicycles. People who had loved ones in World War II lived in fear of a Western Union delivery boy approaching their doors because they knew the dreaded message was going to change their lives forever. Receiving personalized telegrams, the students then write how they think their families would react to such a shocking communication from the government.

To the Parents of John Smith,

I regret to inform you that your son, John Smith, was killed in action on 28th June, 1944, near Lorraine, France. On behalf of the President of the United States and a grateful nation, we extend to you our deepest sympathies.

Sincerely yours,
General George S. Patton
Commanding General
U.S. Third Army

For this part of the writing project, students no longer focus on just their own private thoughts and reactions; their attention must shift to the tormented thoughts of their loved ones as they grapple with the terrifying contents of these telegrams.

When my Mother would receive my "Death Notice" she would be very upset to the point of not being able to cry, not understanding my missing growing up. We were very close; I am a large piece of her heart as she is of mine.

Kurt

My parents would be so upset that they would never change my bedroom; they would keep it as it is in hopes that through some miracle I would come home. They would cry and be very upset for weeks to come.

Sue

To the Parents of Tom Miller,

Your son, Tom Miller, was wounded in battle on 28th June 1944, near Lorraine, France. His wounds are serious but not life

threatening. A member of your local Red Cross unit will be contacting you in the near future to update you on your son's condition.
Sincerely yours,
General George S. Patton
Commanding General
U.S. Third Army

My entire family would be very upset until they could find out how seriously I'm wounded. My Mom would go crazy and my Dad would try to be strong for everyone but he would be very upset also but would try to hide his feelings. They would not rest until they heard from the Red Cross.

Steve

If I was wounded and my parents had no information, they would freak. They would demand to know how seriously I was hurt, and they would want to know that right away. They would be so upset and wouldn't know what to do.

Eric

To the Parents of Harry Farlow,
Your son, Harry Farlow, is listed as missing in action following an engagement with enemy troops on 28th June 1944, near Lorraine, France. Through information received by my command, it is believed that enemy forces have captured your son. Every effort is being made to obtain more information from the International Red Cross. We will keep you updated as new information becomes available.
Sincerely yours,
General George S. Patton
Commanding General
U.S. Third Army

My parents would be terrified; I think my mom would try to go to the battle site. They would not be able to sleep and I would be the same way. My brother and I are very close and I know he would be very upset. My family would never stop looking for me.

Penny

My parents would be very upset to find out that I was missing and possibly captured by German troops. Both of them would cry and not want to believe the telegram.

They would call a government official to try and get some definite information. I don't think they would ever fully recover from this unless they received some kind of definite confirmation about my condition.

Peter

These are just a few examples of the insightful creative writing that my learning-support students have produced with this project. As an amateur historian, I have talked to hundreds of World War II veterans, and three common combat recollections invariably emerge: the terrible din of battle, the revolting smell, and the guilt experienced because they survived while others died. Amazingly, without ever having set one foot on a battlefield, these students often make the same observations in their writing.

Each year the continued success of this project never ceases to amaze me. Incorporating a lesson that integrates their present lives with people and events of the past has made this course more relevant to my students and consequently has inspired them to be more inquisitive and creative. The famous quote of George Santayana is prominently displayed in the front of our classroom to remind all of us why it is so important to study history: Those who cannot remember the past are condemned to repeat it. I like to believe that by putting my students in the cross hairs of the past and the present, we can zero in on a better future.

Although the results of the battlefield project have never been disappointing, there have been other occasions when I tried to implement what I thought were good lesson plans only to have them fall flat when actually put into practice. Such disappointment is inevitable but doesn't necessarily mean that an idea is without merit; it may just indicate a need for some fine-tuning. Another thing to remember is that each class is different: What might work with one group will not always be equally successful with a different group. When first working with special education youngsters, a teacher encounters a lot of trial and error in attempting to formulate the best plans to promote the most learning for all students.

Sometimes a spontaneous lesson prompted by current events or a common concern may be just as effective as one created with much thought and planning. A few years ago a trial was making headlines because two eyewitnesses were giving conflicting testimony. A few of my students wondered how the accounts of two people observing the same event could differ so much. They were about to find out!

Two days later when they came to class, a video camera was set up in the back of the room. I explained that the lesson was being recorded because an administrator, who was unable to be present, wanted to see what I was teaching. Approximately ten minutes into that day's lesson, our high school librarian walked into class and stood next to me while discussing a new library book. Since he was a frequent visitor, the students didn't pay too much attention to us. During his short visit, he handed me a pen and then wrote his name and a three-digit number on the blackboard. Before leaving, he erased everything he had written.

I turned to the class and said, "Now you've just seen what Mr. Piscitelli and I did in front of you. Suppose you were summoned into court as witnesses to this event. How many of you could describe what took place?" I proceeded to give each student a questionnaire concerning the brief episode that had just transpired in their presence. The following questions were asked:

1. Describe what the librarian was wearing – color of his shirt, tie, pants, socks, and shoes.
2. Did he have anything in his shirt pocket?
3. Did he give me anything? If so, what was it and what color was it?
4. Did he write on the board? If so, what did he write?
5. What were we discussing?
6. When he entered the room, did he just walk in or did he knock?
7. On which wrist did he wear his watch?
8. Was he wearing glasses?
9. Was he wearing any rings on his fingers? If so, describe each one.
10. When he left the room, did he open the door with his left or right hand?

When the videotape was viewed, the "witnesses" were astounded by the indisputable results; answers, for the most part, were way off the mark. They remembered some facts correctly, but, overall, there was a great deal of variation among their answers. This was a real learning experience for most of them, and these former students still remark how this lesson gave them a new perspective on how people can view the same event in different ways.

The offhand remark *"I can't wait until I'm eighteen, and I can live on my own!"* prompted the spontaneous development of not just a lesson, but eventually a whole course entitled Job Preparation. This addition to the curriculum, designed to be a real-life experience course, covers such topics as checking accounts, job applications, resume writing, unions, job interviews and many other practical post-graduation concerns.

Further conversation with this senior, *Homo sapiens iknowitallus*, revealed some rather alarming misconceptions about the feasibility of supporting oneself at the tender age of eighteen. Asked how much he thought independent living would cost, this young man's gross underestimation indicated he – and probably most of his classmates – needed a reality check. I told the entire class that the next day we would begin a *Living on Your Own* project and that they should bring in classified ads from the local newspaper.

The first part of this project requires students to interview an apartment complex manager and to acquire a sample lease. It doesn't take long for these soon-to-be graduates to realize more than a friendly hello is required to rent an apartment. Their vocabulary and reality expands as they begin to encounter such obstacles as security deposits, financial references, and income information – all basic needs for signing a lease.

Next, the students become "renters" of a hypothetical unfurnished apartment consisting of a bedroom, kitchen/dining room combination, living room and bath. As a group, they compile a list of items deemed necessary to furnish and comfortably complete each room. Using sales ads, classified ads, or the Internet, each individual is responsible for locating and "buying" these goods. Mom or Dad may donate a maximum of ten items as long as that parent initials his or her consent. A final tabulation of all costs shocks most students, especially the kids with jobs who realize now that their incomes do not come close to supporting an independent lifestyle. Reality begins to sink in. By the end of this project, the general student consensus is best summed up by one young man's remarks in his concluding paragraph:

Most people my age don't really think about the costs of living on your own. It's hard to imagine how expensive it is. I never thought it would be so much to pay for furniture, food, and rent. This project was a real eye opener because it proved to me that I need to save my money if I want to live on my own after high school. I already asked my mom if she would pay my rent for me and she said No! I sort of knew her answer to begin with!

Positive feedback is not always immediately forthcoming. While chaperoning our school's prom, I had a chance to chat with Tom, to whom I had previously taught this unit.

"To be honest, Mr. Riffle, I thought the unit on budgeting money was really stupid. I only completed it for the grade."

" And now, how do you feel about it?" I queried, sensing what was coming next.

"Following graduation, my financial situation was a disaster! I decided to give your stupid method a try and, to my surprise, it really worked!"

Clapping him on the back, I chuckled. "Of course it works! Why do you think I spend time teaching it? Sometimes, Tom, the best teacher is the real world; my job was to prepare you. I guess I did – eventually!"

Group projects also help to vary the daily routine and promote cooperation and responsibility among students. They have to depend on each other's skills and work habits to successfully complete such an endeavor. *Starting Your Own Business* is a project I use in economics to give students basic knowledge about starting and maintaining a company. Hoping to create a realistic and more interesting way to present the material, I developed the following steps:

Step One – A projected product/service must be created that can be further developed – if so desired – into a viable commodity for extra credit. An advertising campaign, complete with logo, print, video, and radio advertisements must be designed to promote the new business.

Step Two – Students describe in detail the work area needed to complete fully the company's work. They list items such as supplies, capital, and work stations necessary to run the business successfully.

Step Three – Class members list the number of employees that need to be hired. Each worker's required job skills must be defined in detail. No worker may be described as general labor.

Step Four – Students develop an appropriate job application for the prospective employees. This precise form must contain general information plus specific information unique to the company's needs.

Step Five – Students develop a list of interview questions to help the company hire only qualified employees. They then divide the questions into three categories:

1. Personnel Information

2. Past Employment Record

3. Specific Questions (pertaining to this company)

Step Six – Groups develop a list of company safety rules and procedures. These regulations are divided into two areas:

1. General Safety and Procedure Policies

2. Specific Work Station Policies

Step Seven – Teams establish a company pay scale, listing probable earnings for all people mentioned in **Step Two**. The employee's value to the company is reflected in the pay scale.

Step Eight – Students draw up a realistic list of employee benefits, being aware that any benefit offered to the workers cuts into the profit margin.

Step Nine- As a conclusion, each student writes a one-page summary explaining what was learned while working on this project.

Students seem to be more motivated to work on a project when they are allowed some leeway in choosing which parts they want to be responsible for rather than having the teacher always determine the parameters. Individual skills and talents are better utilized, and each member of the group becomes a confident contributor.

No matter what kind of lesson or project is employed, it should be as interesting and relevant as possible to the students. For example, when covering the American Civil War era, I literally and figuratively try to whet their appetites and serve them an authentic Civil War meal. The food is terrible and there are no compliments to the chef, but this activity helps history come alive and creates more interest than just reading about the soldiers' diet.

Interesting anecdotes concerning my great-grandfather, who was a prisoner in the infamous Andersonville Prison in Georgia, are interspersed throughout my lectures. After he returned from the war, this lucky survivor related many stories to his family about the horrendous living conditions in this southern prison camp. I pass on my historically rich inheritance to my students as they listen with rapt attention. Although transporting them back in time is impossible, they are asked to imagine, as an example, what they would do to survive if the drinking water in camp were too polluted for safe consumption. Although they come up with some clever ideas, they are taken aback to learn these men actually managed to stay alive by drinking "clean" rainwater that collected in the hoof prints of the mule and the wheel ruts of the wagon that regularly passed through the camp to pick up dead bodies!

There are times lessons spill out of the classroom and reap special and unexpected rewards beyond the mere mastery of subject matter. One history project I use includes a section offering an option of constructing a model of a World War II plane, ship, or tank. One student and his disabled father built a model of the USS Arizona to complete this phase of the project. This boy's dad couldn't share many of the normal father-and-son activities like playing catch, riding a bike, or taking a hike in the woods, but this activity leveled the playing field. Later, the dad told me it was a great experience for both of them.

Another World War II project requires students to interview their grandparents, or, if that isn't possible, anyone over the age of seventy. They develop a set of questions pertaining to popular music, movies, sports, fashions and many other topics that enable them to delve into the early years of their grandparents' lives. This questionnaire has not only provided them with glimpses of life in another era, but has also reinforced intergenerational relationships. One grandfather called me and thanked me for the interview questions because for the first time his grandson had actually sat down and talked to him!

Keeping the lines of communication open with students is also an important goal for teachers. There still isn't a better complement to the development of a favorable learning environment than positive, daily exchanges between teachers and their pupils. Even when implementing an ordinary lesson on an ordinary day, a teacher makes learning more memorable and fun by encouraging light-hearted interaction with the students.

I taught a young man named Jack, a.k.a. "Jumping Jack Flash," who definitely wasn't applying himself to the pursuit of academic goals. One day while teaching 19th Century American History, the term *popular sovereignty* was introduced into the lesson. I told the class that, for whatever reason, students always have a tough time learning this term. Jack put his hand up and declared, "I'll remember it."

Wanting to hold him to this promise, I guaranteed Jack a free lunch if he could remember the definition for the entire school year. To make the bargain official, we signed a hastily written agreement – a custom between my students and me whenever such a wager is struck. On the test that included *popular sovereignty*, I put in parentheses behind the term "Ask Jack!" Naturally, Jack had accurately identified the term and was so thrilled to have his name associated with a test question that he took the exam home and showed his parents!

Periodically throughout the year, I quizzed Jack on this term in class, and he always knew the correct answer. Surprisingly, he started to apply himself in all areas of the course, dramatically increasing his overall grade. Imagine: All this came about because of a positive interaction between Jack and myself over a pre-Civil War term!

Another silly trick saved the day for Debi, a good student who, for some reason, could not remember that Leif Ericson was Eric the Red's son. It seemed like a simple fact, but Debi just couldn't get it straight. When I asked her the day before the test which finger she used to dial a phone, she held out her right index finger. While telling her to keep that finger extended, I pulled out a bottle of red nail polish from my desk drawer, and, as Debi laughed hysterically, painted that nail red. For emphasis, I loudly repeated, "Red comes first because he's the father."

The next day while taking the test, she held up her finger with the brightly painted nail in a victorious gesture. Years later when I saw her again, I asked her the very same question. She wiggled her index finger, smiled, and still gave me the correct answer. The red nail polish had long since been removed, but not her memory of Eric the Red!

In biology class I always have kids who think snakes are born for one reason – to bite humans. This misconception, of course, causes them to fear snakes. I teasingly tell these students that every morning the snakes have a staff meeting to discuss which people they're going to bite that day!

To emphasize the point that snakes usually bite humans only when they feel endangered, I coax two snake-fearing students to the front of the class to role-play. One dubious volunteer lies on the floor on his back while the other participant stands over the "snake." The person on the floor has a snake's-eye view of a human. Asked if he/she would *want* to attack something that much bigger unless feeling threatened, most participants laugh and admit they would not.

Congratulations are definitely deserved if you have discovered successful methods to boost the attention and interest levels of your students, but be sure to carefully scout the learning landscape for any lurking pitfalls that can impede progress and drain enthusiasm. For instance, testing can be a major drawback for children with learning disabilities. These students should have the opportunity to acquire enough points to score a "C" or higher for the first marking period. In fact, no child who is trying his or her best should receive a lower grade at any time throughout the year. Homework, effort, and attitude should be factored into the marking system along with test grades.

The use of study guides is one practice that can be implemented to produce successful testing outcomes. To help students retain information, teachers can distribute blank guides to be completed for a grade. The day before the test, students turn in their study guides and receive another with the correct answers typed in caps and bold print to facilitate reading.

The actual test should be based primarily on the study guide. The entire class period the day before the test should be devoted to reviewing the material and eliminating any misconceptions or questions the students might have. Occasionally, students can create their own test if the class is split in half and each group makes up a set of questions based on the covered material. As the students share their questions, they decide which ones will become the basis of the test. Naturally, the teacher can add anything of importance the students may have missed.

Testing learning-disabled students can be especially difficult due to the wide range of abilities existing in one class. Sometimes it's advantageous to create two different tests – easy and challenging versions that cover the same material. The easy test could consist of matching (five words in a group), multiple choice, and true and false questions; the harder test could include short-answer questions. The front page of both tests must have a similar appearance to prevent the students from easily noting the differences.

This dual testing method might be more time-consuming for the teacher, but the system is undeniably fairer for the kids. Granted, giving the easier test to everyone is much simpler, but such a test would not challenge the more advanced students. As the year progresses, the students taking the easy test can graduate to the more difficult exams as their levels of confidence improve. Of course, no method is foolproof, and, sooner or later, kids compare notes, and complaints arise concerning why certain classmates have easier tests. There is no set answer for that question; you'll just have to be creative with your answer!

Due to reading disabilities, some students need to have their tests read to them in another room. Since they might be self-conscious about leaving the room, this relocation must be accomplished as unobtrusively as possible. I once had a young man who refused to leave the room to have his test read; he preferred failing the test to letting his classmates know he had a reading deficiency. To salvage his pride, he was given a practice test while his classmates took the actual test. Later, he had the regular test read to him during a study hall.

When correcting tests, all teachers should be mindful of any questions answered incorrectly by a large percentage of the class. If this happens – and it will – that question should be eliminated from the scoring process. Obviously, it was either a poorly worded question or the concept was not taught to achieve mastery. Too many low grades on a test might indicate the teacher made errors in presenting the material. There are two options: either count the grades or create a new test.

My suggestion is to stand in front of the students with the tests in your hands and tell them that you created a poor test. With dramatic flair, tear up the tests and toss them in the trashcan. Review the material again, and then administer a new test. This type of overt display earns respect from students because many of them have never seen a teacher openly admit a mistake. How refreshing for the students to regard their teacher as a *real* person, *Homo sapiens imperfectus!*

Periodically, a student panics or procrastinates when faced with a large assignment. Even though an extended time period is allotted to complete an extensive project, some kids feel overwhelmed before they even start. For instance, one of my history units is comprised of twenty-four different segments. One girl who had emotional problems took a look at it, rolled her eyes, and lamented that it was too much to do and that she absolutely would not be able to complete this project on time. I told her I understood and reached for her packet. I cut out the first sentence and told her to complete just that one. She smiled and proceeded to finish the first requirement quickly. I then cut out the second assignment and so on. Ultimately, she handed in her completed packet on time! Going from "can't do" to "can do" was simply a matter of dividing a lengthy project into less threatening incremental steps.

By all means, a job well done should not go unnoticed. Learning-disabled students need an inordinate amount of encouragement to keep striving to do their best work. They need to hear regularly words of praise. A teacher should write notes on their assignments, give them a *high five*, or offer simple rewards. The manner in which the kudos are delivered is not as important as the sincerity and meaningfulness to the recipient. Of course, there are always exceptions!

Many years ago I was working with two little boys who had both scored a hundred percent on a test. I marked their papers in the following way:

John 100<u>% Super!!</u> Bob 100<u>% Super!</u>

Bob went to tears, and I didn't have a clue as to why he was crying. I asked him what was wrong, and he said, "John has a better score than I do." I assured him the scores were absolutely the same. Still not appeased by my answer, Bob asked, "Why does John have two of those lines, and I only have one?" I still didn't get it until he showed me that I had put two exclamation points on John's test and only one on his!

Years later I again handed back two perfect papers and the one boy said, "How come Jack has two lines under his 100% and I only have one?" Thirty-four years after the first incident, the situation arose again, and this time it involved a pair of high school kids – not second graders. Talk about *déjà vu*! I finally learned my lesson; to this day, I write all one hundred percents exactly alike.

• • • • •

During the summer of 2001, the Disney Corporation invited the previous year's American Teacher Award winners to Florida for a weeklong seminar on creative teaching practices and techniques. While attending the numerous meetings, we were given orange pens with Disney Institute printed on them. I remarked to the people in charge that I loved those pens because they were large enough to fit my oversized "paws." All week long I was teased because in all the years they had worked with ATA winners, no one had ever complimented them on their pens.

That Christmas someone at Disney sent me an anonymous "gift." The package contained dozens of Disney Institute pens. One of my students spied the pens and expressed a desire to own one of them, too. Coincidentally, he had just moments ago received a 100% on a history test, so I told him he had rightfully earned a pen and ceremoniously placed one on his desk. I overlooked the significance of this gesture, but the other kids didn't. Three other students who had "aced" the same test reminded me of their *A*'s and also desired pens. Owning an orange Disney pen soon became a source of pride.

I was forced to quickly formulate a rule governing the awarding of this instantly popular commodity: To earn a pen, a student had to score 90% or higher on a major test in any of my courses. The number of students receiving *A*'s increased, and, if for some reason I forgot to present one, the student I missed quickly reminded me of my oversight. Even one girl in another teacher's learning support class asked me if she could be eligible for a pen. I told her the rule and promised her she could have a pen if she earned it. Sadly, three weeks later this student's mother died from cancer. All rules were forgotten; she was given a pen.

Another motivational tradition I have instituted is called "Riffle's Raiders," a yearlong program designed to promote continued academic progress whereby students compete only against themselves and not against each other. The rules are very simple: Students must improve their first-quarter grade in each successive marking period that follows. For example, if a student's quarter grades for the year are 72%, 73%, 75%, and 76%, that person automatically qualifies for this end-of-the-year activity. The exception is the student who scores an *A* first quarter. This child must maintain an *A* average for all four marking periods.

Throughout the course of the year, many students inquire about their grades and strive to achieve a higher percentage than the previous marking period. At the conclusion of each quarter, the names of those students still eligible for this award are posted, and the final winners are announced on the last day of school. Their reward is a free luncheon at a local buffet restaurant, a framed certificate, and a photograph celebrating the event. This luncheon, also attended by teachers, parents, and administration, has become a proud tradition.

Occasionally, no matter what elaborate attempts have been made to establish a favorable learning environment, some children shut down for no apparent reason and refuse to do any work in class. Finding out what is causing this apparent lack of effort is essential. Frequently, a stressful situation outside of school is responsible for a child's poor academic performance.

For instance, when I noticed one of my student's grades dropping dramatically one quarter, I began to observe her more closely. She appeared to be extremely tired all the time, and, eventually, keeping her awake in class was almost impossible. When this problem was finally addressed, I learned that her father took her to a bar every night so he had someone *reliable* to drive him home after a few hours of heavy drinking. Obviously lacking good parenting skills and common sense, he also overlooked the fact that his designated driver was only fifteen years old, a full year under the legal driving age in Pennsylvania! Confronted about this serious situation, the father conceded that maybe having his daughter drive him home wasn't such a good idea, and then, as an afterthought, added, "But that's okay because I'm a better driver drunk anyway!"

A teacher cannot "fix" every negative aspect of a child's life, but every teacher does have the ability to listen. Students do not always care about what you know or what you want them to know; but they do always want to know that you care. By whatever means possible, a committed teacher must make that special effort or find that extra time to show students that their well-being is his or her primary concern.

Become a teacher who truly listens, and students will listen to you – and learn!

CHAPTER 5

"A smooth sea never made a skilled mariner."
... English proverb

Throughout my career in the classroom, I have confronted many strange and unexpected situations. Some circumstances were humorous and inspirational while others were frightening, inexplicable, and even tragic. A few years ago we experienced such a bizarre set of events over a two-day period that I didn't cover a single lesson on those days! As I tried to resolve one situation, my aide held down the fort with the rest of the troops. Just as I almost had one problem settled, lo and behold, another crisis cropped up! At the end of the second stressful day, I was utterly frustrated and mentally exhausted. Wearily resting my head in my hands, I sighed heavily, "And all I do is teach!"

There is no magical formula to follow to ensure that every day in the classroom will be an unqualified success. Even if it were possible to acquire outstanding teaching skills and credentials, to create the perfect classroom environment and the most stimulating lesson plans, and to possess and display unlimited enthusiasm, such an educational nirvana would still be susceptible to the *unpredictability factor.* This ever-present component of life has no respect for your daily educational agenda and will occasionally jolt you out of your academic complacency and test your mettle as a teacher.

Bud

An extremely scary situation evolved when I was a student teacher in Philadelphia. A fifth-grade student named Bud became a casual acquaintance by calling out a friendly hello to me from the hallway every day after school. I could have set my watch by this daily ritual initiated by a seemingly happy and outgoing boy.

One day when he passed by my room without greeting me, I called out, "Hi Bud!" He just grunted and kept on walking. I thought *Oh, well, he isn't having a good day.* Shortly thereafter, I heard someone screaming obscenities in the corridor. Sprinting out of my room and up the entire length of the hallway, I was horrified to find Bud viciously beating a female staff member. Blood covered her face, and her clothes were disheveled and torn. I grabbed him by the shoulders, and, cat-like, he turned and pounced on me.

Physically, he was just an average fifth grader, and although I'm 6' 6", I was never in a tougher fight. He kicked me repeatedly and tried to claw at my face with his flailing hands. I managed to yank his face towards the wall and to pin him there securely with my body. He was calling me every vulgar term he could think of, and then – as if someone had thrown a switch – he stopped.

I felt the tension drain out of his arms, and he started to cry. Cautiously, I backed away from him because I distrusted this startling change in his demeanor and thought he might attack me again. I walked him over to a bench where he lay down and went to sleep. I was mystified and had no idea what had just transpired. Even more puzzling was his normal, friendly greeting the next time I saw him: "Hi, Mr. Riffle. How are you?" He acted as if nothing had ever happened!

The following year, while riding a commuter train to graduate school in Philadelphia, I recognized Bud a few rows in front of me. Curiosity overwhelmed me and led me to the empty seat beside him. I had to ask him about that incident. Since I was no longer teaching at his school, I figured he'd tell me the truth. I sat with him and discussed mundane matters until that situation could casually be brought into the conversation.

Bud looked at me with a quizzical expression on his face, smiled, and said, "Are you kidding? I'd never fight you; you'd kill me!" He wasn't joking. He had absolutely no idea what I was talking about. This was one mystery that would have to remain unsolved, but it always left me feeling uneasy and wondering what would happen if someone with a larger physique lost control with a seizure-like disorder.

Susan

One of the funniest incidents involved my son Matt when he was a young teacher. He had an emotionally disturbed little girl named Susan in his second-grade class. Susan carried a small stuffed horse with her named Charley. And just like Mary and her little lamb of nursery-rhyme fame, everywhere that Susan went, Charley went, too.

One day Susan was acting inappropriately in class. Matt told her to behave herself and to stop bothering everyone else. As he turned to write on the board, Susan said, "F_ _ _ you!"

Matt whirled around and sternly inquired, "What did you say?"

Susan replied, "It wasn't me! It was Charley!"

Matt told me it took all he could do not to laugh. She kept insisting it was Charley, so Matt wisely compromised. "Okay, Charley is suspended from school!"

A letter informing Susan's parents of the pending suspension was sent home. Unlike Mary's more docile lamb, Charley was not allowed back in school for two weeks!

Jerry

Perhaps one of the most intriguing youngsters I've ever known was Jerry, a child diagnosed as ADHD with autistic tendencies. Although I've been in his presence numerous times, I've never actually had the privilege of teaching him. My daughter Rebecca worked with him during his early school years and found him both fascinating and challenging to teach.

Jerry, like many children with autistic characteristics, displays incredible knowledge about one particular subject. In his case, it pertained to wiring installed by our local cable company. When our new elementary school was being wired for cable TV, Jerry was an avid observer. He dogged the technicians from place to place, never missing a thing they did. In fact, Rebecca told me that whenever the cable company arrived, Jerry always stopped in the middle of his own activities to concentrate on what the men were doing. If Rebecca knew they were scheduled to be in her building that day, she did whatever was humanly possible to conceal that fact from Jerry.

About a year after the new school opened, the cable company returned to fix a problem with the system. The technicians were looking for a junction box, which they couldn't seem to locate. Once again, despite Rebecca doing her utmost to conceal their presence in her hallway, the ever-observant Jerry soon spied the workmen with their rolled-up blueprints and stepladder.

As the men kept repositioning the ladder in order to remove different ceiling panels, Jerry became exceedingly curious about what they were searching for and continually quizzed them about what they were trying to find. The men were tolerant of his insistent questions, but really never answered him. Finally, after enduring Jerry's unending bombardment of inquiries, one exasperated workman blurted, "The junction box!"

Jerry gleefully replied, "Why didn't you say so before? I know where it is!"

The men looked at Rebecca with skeptical expressions on their faces. She said, "If he says he knows where it is, he probably does."

Jerry eagerly reached for the nearest man's hand and immediately guided him over to one corner of the classroom. Like picking out a suspect in a police line-up, he pointed to a specific ceiling tile and said with certainty, "It's that one!"

The ladder was once again reset so that this particular tile could be removed in order to find out if the mystery junction box was indeed above it. Excited at the sight of the ladder, Jerry begged to climb the ladder and remove the tile himself. Rebecca stopped him as he began to scramble up the first two steps and told him only the workmen were allowed to mount the ladder. The panel was swiftly removed and – sure enough – there was the elusive junction box!

The cable crew was astounded, but Jerry acted like it was no big deal. One of the workmen jokingly asked the youngster if he would like to join the company and work for them.

Jerry responded, "I'm only six years old!"

The workmen pretended to confer with each other and then said, "Okay, how about when you're older?"

Jerry pleaded, "Would I have a cable shirt and climb the ladder, too?"

The workers sealed the deal with *high fives* all around.

Possibly, these men were convinced they had just met a gifted child, which in fact Jerry is in certain ways. Naturally, if they had seen him in another situation, they would have been very confused by his inappropriate behavior. ADHD children have a wide range of abilities and disabilities all at the same time.

Jeremy

About halfway through one school year, I was informed that a new student, who had been severely brain damaged in an accident, would be placed in some of my classes. To prepare my students for his arrival, I shared some background information about the boy's mishap and the resulting injuries. When I had finished telling them only what I thought they needed to know, I noticed almost everyone was staring at Jeremy.

Jeremy was usually a good-natured boy, always willing to volunteer his help, but when I asked the group if any were acquainted with the new student, Jeremy only reluctantly raised his hand. I really didn't think too much about his odd reaction and had totally forgotten it by the time I was summoned to the principal's office the next morning.

Once inside the door, I was instantly sucked into an emotional maelstrom. An agitated couple sat across the desk from the principal.

The father's glowering face indicated he was furious. He ranted that his son was not to be placed in the same class with a certain other student and threatened to sue the school district if the situation wasn't immediately rectified. I stood quietly trying to figure out who they were and what was happening.

When this tirade ended, the principal quickly introduced me to Jeremy's parents and briefly summarized the problem. Before his accident, this new student had attacked their son for no apparent reason, causing permanent damage to Jeremy's one eye. There was also a pending lawsuit concerning this incident.

I now understood the principal's dilemma: Course schedules were set by this time, the new student was restricted to certain classes because he was still undergoing intensive therapy, and Jeremy's parents didn't want their own son inconvenienced to effect this necessary separation. I wasn't sure Solomon could solve this mess, but maybe Jeremy could! As soon as he joined us, I asked him if he could tolerate the situation for the balance of the week in order for us to work out the scheduling problems. Jeremy agreed to this compromise, but only until the following Monday.

The next morning the brain-damaged student was wheeled into my room. The last time Jeremy had seen this boy he had been a physically fit teenager, and now – exhibiting childlike mental and emotional characteristics – he was imprisoned by a wheelchair. Speechless, Jeremy just sat there and stared at him. The injured boy stared back, but without any recollection of the troubled history they shared.

For the remainder of the week, Jeremy warily observed his former opponent from a distance. It was outwardly apparent he was waging an inner battle, but having a difficult time identifying the enemy. By Friday, Jeremy was willing to call a truce. He realized this wasn't the same boy who had deliberately hurt him, and it was going to be all right for them to be classmates.

In the weeks that followed, old boundary lines were crossed. Jeremy eventually sat next to the boy and helped him with his homework. It was also commonplace to see the two of them laughing as Jeremy pushed him in his wheelchair to lunch. Besides taking on the job of caretaker, Jeremy had also acquired a new friend and a new outlook on life.

Dion

Dion was a young man who had suffered more sorrow than anyone at any age should have to endure. In the short span of two and a half years, this seventeen-year-old boy lost his father, mother, grandmother, sister and two brothers. His family unit of eight disintegrated into two in that short time. I was with him through all the deaths but one. It's hard enough to console a young person who has lost any loved one, but what do you say when untimely deaths claim six close relatives in such a brief period of time?

Dion's situation totally unnerved me. I ran out of comforting words, and, any wisdom I could usually offer, seemed woefully inadequate in the face of such overwhelming loss. Despite this fracturing of his familial support system, Dion somehow waded through all of this tragedy without falling apart emotionally. Teachers cannot always make things right again for their students, but they can be supportive when things go wrong.

Paul

One afternoon a loud argument erupted in the hallway, and the angry voices sounded familiar. Prepared to play referee, I rushed out of my room and discovered two of my students face-to-face, black-to-white, embroiled in a heated dispute. Quickly defusing a potentially explosive situation, I guided them to a private room to find out what had triggered this display of unruly behavior. These two guys had always been good friends, and I couldn't imagine what had happened to change their solid relationship.

Paul, the black student, was most upset. Apparently the white student had told a racial joke, and Paul was offended. I curtly informed both boys we would settle this argument after school in my classroom. I realized that resolving this matter would pose a dilemma because our school has a small minority population, and I didn't want Paul to think a white teacher let a white kid off too lightly.

These two former friends faced each other again at three o'clock. Since Paul was the one offended, I felt he should hand out the punishment. He resisted taking that responsibility upon himself. Unwilling to compromise this point, I insisted his input would be a requirement for settling their differences and just cautioned him to make the punishment fit the crime. The white kid was notably upset and apologized profusely, but to no avail.

The punishment meted out was four detentions and one day of in-school suspension. Everyone agreed to these terms. As the three of us stood up, Paul said, "There is just one more thing – you also lost my friendship." The other boy was crushed because he probably would have served ten detentions to avoid that particular consequence.

Paul meant what he said and, unfortunately, remained unforgiving. In the last two years of school, I never saw them interact again. I thought time would heal the wound and that their former strong bond would prevail, but sadly – in this case – there wasn't a happy ending.

Tom

In the spring of the year 2000, I was sitting at my desk when a firm knock on the door diverted my attention from the mound of paperwork I was feebly attempting to organize. Recognizing my visitor as a former student and badly needing a mental respite, I motioned for him to enter the room. In strode Tom, a 1991 graduate I had never expected to come back to school voluntarily. While attending high school, he had sat in the principal's office as often as he did in my classroom! His cocky attitude had kept him in constant trouble with students and staff alike. I couldn't imagine what important matter had brought him back to my desk nine years later.

Without hesitation, Tom walked over to me and shook my hand. He said, "I came here to apologize to you, Mr. Riffle, because when I was a student here, I was a real jerk. All you ever did was try to help me, and I'm sorry for all the grief I caused."

I was momentarily stunned into silence – a state that is not commonplace for me. I never would have ever expected an apology from Tom for any reason! I smiled broadly and said, "Apology accepted, but what prompted your decision to come back and make this admission to me?"

"Do you remember how you used to tell us that real life experience is the best teacher? Well," he continued as I nodded, "you were right. I got out of high school and I thought I knew everything. Then I found out I didn't know anything. It took me a while, but I finally smartened up. I'm now a certified mechanic, and I start computer school this summer."

Tom sincerely thanked me, shook my hand again, and left, leaving my aide and I dazed. As the door closed behind him, she mused, "You never know about these kids, do you? Here's a young man whom you haven't seen in nine years, and he comes back to say he's sorry. That has to make your day!"

It did, and the pile of paperwork in front of me seemed a little less daunting.

Donald and David

Every once in a while, a situation that defies a plausible explanation arises. As a young teacher, I worked in a room with severely retarded youngsters. One set of identical twin boys were both mentally retarded *and* emotionally disturbed. However, these two kids were supremely gifted with the ability to create havoc in a classroom! To save my sanity, I had to find a surefire way to eliminate their rowdy behavior.

Advice: When all else fails, sit back, observe, and analyze the situation! In this case, I noticed a pattern of calmer behavior whenever the boys were seated in a certain area of the room. Gradually, I realized the reason for their improved conduct was not based on *where* they were seated, but upon *what* they were seated.

Whenever they became hyperactive, to calm them down I merely had them sit on soft pillows! They could be running around the room like wild banshees, but when made to sit on those pillows, they both became manageable. It was astounding to watch this transformation unfold in a matter of seconds. Don't ask me why this method was successful because as the kids say, "I ain't got a clue." The important thing was that it worked!

Frank

Whenever a new family moved into our neighborhood, my wife and I made it a habit to introduce ourselves and welcome them to the community. As we exchanged pleasantries with one particular couple, the fact that I was a special education teacher came into the conversation. Both parents seemed unusually interested in my profession. In fact, the casual conversation quickly began to focus exclusively on my teaching expertise. Just as we were ready to return home, our new friends invited us to meet their youngest son.

Frank was summoned from the rec room. Noticing he was all decked out in his Phillies hat and shirt, I discussed baseball with him for a few minutes and then he returned to the game he was watching. His mother turned to me and asked, "How old do you think he is?"

I responded, "Nine or ten."

She said, "He's seventeen."

I couldn't believe what I had just heard; he looked like a normal ten-year-old.

The mother explained that at the age of seventeen, Frank had not yet experienced puberty. I was asked what I thought could be wrong with their son. Before I responded, they assured me that they had already taken him to various specialists and no one seemed to have an answer. I told them I certainly wasn't capable of rendering a diagnosis although I was fairly sure his growth problem was due to some type of hormone deficiency.

I asked their permission to contact Dr. Robert Buckalew, a former professor of mine at Kutztown University. He was a brilliant man whose opinion I greatly valued. I told the parents that if Dr. Buckalew didn't know the answer, he most likely would be able to recommend someone who could help them.

A meeting was arranged, and, as I had surmised, Dr. Buckalew directed the family to an endocrinologist who put Frank into a cutting-edge program. His body gradually began to mature, and he added three more inches to his height. Frank is now in his late thirties and leads a normal adult life.

• • • • •

Unfortunately, not all problems have a simple solution or are even solvable. Suicide is one of the leading causes of death among people under the age of twenty-five. The number of young people ending their own lives has risen dramatically over the past few decades. Sadly, this alarming trend did not circumvent the students who once sat in my own classroom. I have taught eight students who took their own lives and several others who attempted suicide.

Bob

Bob, a troubled young man, was the innocent victim of a dysfunctional home environment. His mother had had a serious mental breakdown, and he was emotionally estranged from his father. During his senior year, he discovered his father having an affair with another woman. He knew he couldn't tell his mother due to her unstable state of mind, so he internalized the situation for several months. One day, so distraught and overwhelmed by his secret burden, he broke down and told me the entire story.

I did what I could to counsel him, but the problem was beyond my expertise at the time. He was eighteen, and I was only twenty-five. Dealing with Bob was extremely difficult, and the situation only worsened as the year progressed. Each day spent with him, I never knew what type of emotional situation would confront me. Unfortunately, school districts didn't have mental health specialists at that time to help students deal with emotional crises. Only two years after he graduated, Bob committed suicide.

Harry

Harry, who was from a socially prominent family, had a learning disability and was also involved with illegal drugs. Whenever I called the home, his father acted as if I were bothering him. Harry told me his father basically ignored him and only seemed concerned about his sisters. On occasion kids will feel this way when reality is actually quite different.

However, shortly thereafter, I had a rather eye-opening meeting with Harry's father. The man strode in and literally said, "I'm in a hurry. Where do I sign?"

I tried to tactfully talk to him about his son and his son's problems, but the more I spoke, the more agitated he became. Finally out of frustration I said, "You know your son wants to spend time with you."

His answer was one I will never forget. He said, "I have two daughters who are going to go to college; I don't have time to waste on him!" I was stymied by his heartless explanation and stood mute with anger as he signed the papers and left.

He didn't have to worry about wasting much more time on his son because Harry committed suicide in the family garage two years later. I could only sadly hope that the father hadn't been too busy to attend the funeral.

Simon

Simon was mentally retarded and emotionally unstable. He also had a problem with fine motor skills. The Pennsylvania Dutch might have referred to him as "armselig." He was indeed a poor soul, and I always felt sorry for him. Apparently, though, his teacher didn't share my sentiments. Just before Thanksgiving in 1968, his special education class had a classroom Thanksgiving feast. The teacher charged each student fifty cents to eat the meal. Simon forgot his money, so she made him sit in the cafeteria without food while everyone else had a party. It was a heartless act. I couldn't believe she had ostracized him for this reason. When I confronted her about it, she told me she had taught Simon a valuable lesson. Some lesson! I also learned a lesson; she wasn't fit to teach!

Simon confided in me that he wanted a friend: "If I ever find a friend, I will be the best friend that person ever had!" I told him we were friends, but he pointed out that I was an adult and he wanted a buddy his own age. Who knows what a difference an age-appropriate companion might have made in his life because if there was ever a boy who desperately needed a friend, it was Simon.

He was the youngest of three children, but not even his family could provide Simon the support and acceptance he so desperately sought and never found at school. Ridicule was common at home, too. When the family had dinner in the dining room, he was banished to the kitchen to eat by himself. Frequently, when the family went out for dinner, they were unwilling to have him accompany them and forced him to stay home alone. Surely, this miserable existence did not lay sturdy groundwork for what was to follow.

As his father lay dying from cancer, he informed a totally unprepared Simon that he was now the man of the family and had to take care of everyone. The pressure put on this young man was unbearable. Simon struggled with this problem for two or three years, and, when he couldn't handle it anymore, he took his own life. He was only nineteen at the time of his death.

Whenever suicide is mentioned in class – a subject not included in my curriculum-mandated material – it is given serious attention and frankly discussed with my students. Implausible as it sounds, I am often left with the impression that they don't truly realize the finality of death and that suicide is a permanent solution to a short-term problem. Therefore, I always tell kids that when they confront what seems to be an insurmountable problem to stop and ask themselves this question: *Will this situation still concern me in ten years?* Since the answer to that question is usually *no*, they start to understand that all dilemmas other than death can be worked out.

• • • • •

Samuel

In addition to confronting suicide, you may also have to deal with cases of physical and sexual abuse. One of my mother's special education students was beaten repeatedly by his alcoholic father. In fact, when people visited the home, this boy would be locked in a closet. One day when he came to school, he could barely walk. My mother asked him what was wrong, and he matter-of-factly answered, "My father kicked me in the groin and threw me down the steps!"

The school nurse examined him and verified the story. This was before there were any laws to protect children from abuse. Incredibly, this type of abuse continues, and, sad to say, most children protect their abusive parents from the authorities.

Jane

It is absolutely necessary that children be protected from human animals that prey on their innocence. I strongly believe that the most dangerous animal on earth is the human being that attacks children. Many years ago, I taught a retarded girl named Jane who was a victim of incest. Her father and her two brothers sexually abused her on a regular basis. She once described to me in graphic detail the horrors she endured in her own home.

I checked with the principal to see what could be done to protect this poor child. I was told she would have to contact the police herself because if I initiated the process and she refused to testify, I could be prosecuted. I tried to persuade her to call the police, but she refused, saying, "I don't want my father and brothers to go to jail."

Samantha

I had another retarded child who was routinely beaten with a belt by her parents. I knew this abuse was not hearsay because she wore the evidence on her arms and legs – red welts, obvious trademarks of unrestrained physical assault. Since she was already eighteen years of age, there was nothing I could do to protect her. The child had an IQ of 50, but the new child abuse law inadequately protected her because it was based solely on chronological age; mental age was irrelevant. Our local police chief told me that the only way she could be helped was by filing a complaint against her parents. Since she was retarded, there was no chance of that happening!

The law that made it mandatory to report suspected child abuse was long overdue. This newest law not only protected the child, but also protected the adult who reported the alleged abuse if the claim was determined to be false. One thing that has become very evident to me over the years is that kids have become very knowledgeable about the laws affecting themselves. Occasionally, they will use this knowledge to persecute an innocent person. This new law shielded me from a possible lawsuit when one of my girls tried to have her father arrested for alleged abuse.

Tanya

Tanya vengefully attempted to get back at her father because he had disciplined her by forbidding her to watch TV for one week. She came to my class one day seeming terribly upset and then proceeded to tell me her father had sexually molested her. She asked for my help in seeking protection from him. I notified the principal, and he, in turn, called the local police department.

Since the girl had already told me the entire story, I was asked to sit in on the conversation with Tanya and her counselor. As the story was retold, some significant parts were not related as they had been originally disclosed to me. I didn't say anything, but I did jot down some notes.

In the meantime, the police went to the home and took a statement from Tanya's stunned father. I told our principal that I was concerned because some of her story had changed since hearing the first rendition that morning. We now had some legitimate concerns regarding the authenticity of these charges.

The school brought in another counselor and had Tanya give her account again. Both the girl's counselor and I were also at this second meeting. The story was altered again, and, under gentle questioning, she broke down and told us she had lied because she was mad at her dad.

This type of situation puts everyone in education under extreme pressure because if a parent truly is a predator who attacks children, he or she has to be dealt with severely. On the other hand, if the allegations are proven false, they can still cause irreparable damage to someone's reputation. In this case, the school recommended professional counseling for both the parent and child.

Mike

On the other side of the coin are the effects of parental neglect and indifference. Many years ago, a newborn baby was literally dumped on the doorsteps of a local children's agency. The authorities were unable to locate the mother, so the child was placed in foster care. The caretakers named this newborn baby Mike.

I met Mike when he entered tenth grade. Since I wasn't aware of his home situation, I had no idea that the family of which he so often spoke was pure fantasy. In order to fit in with the other students, he had created an entire family unit in his mind. I discovered the imaginary nature of these relatives while talking to his foster parents.

I distinctly remember asking him to come to our house for Christmas. He thanked me but said, "You know Christmas is for families, and we always go to my grandmother's house for the holidays." He was so convincing that I thought I had misunderstood his foster parents. I called them, and they guaranteed me there was no grandmother in his life and never had been.

Many years later while visiting our local mall, I met Mike again. He had become a big strapping man with a *real* family – a wife and two children. We rambled on about the old days for a few minutes and exchanged photos of our kids. Then he made a strange request.

He asked, "May I hug you?"

"Sure," I replied.

He stepped back and asked, "Are you sure it's okay?"

I said, "Absolutely."

He put his arms around me and we held each other for a long time. When he released me he said, "That's for all you did for me when I was a kid."

Timmy

As a new teacher, I worked with a young boy named Timmy who desperately wanted attention from his father. He and I talked about his home situation at great length. His dad owned a family-run business that usurped most of his time. What spare hours he did have were spent on a golf course. I frequently saw his name on the sports page after he had competed in local amateur tournaments.

During one of our discussions, I asked Timmy what he specifically would like to do with his dad. I learned that he longed for the two of them to build a fort in their backyard. Since Timmy often told me about the tree huts and forts he built on weekends, this wish made perfect sense. The dilemma was how to approach his father; I was only twenty-two at the time with no children of my own, so I had to very gingerly suggest some parenting tips to his dad.

Timmy's father was exceedingly polite to me on the phone but informed me that his business placed severe restraints on his free time. I was very tempted to remonstrate: *Give up one round of golf for your son.* However, I bit my tongue instead, and he finally assured me he would take time to work with Timmy that coming weekend.

I didn't tell Timmy about the impending father-son project until the end of the day on Friday because I was sure he would be so excited that he would stop focusing on his schoolwork. I took him aside just before the final bell. Feeling like Santa Claus on Christmas Eve, I told him what was in store. Ecstatic, forgetting his papers and books, Timmy went flying out the door.

I was very anxious to see Timmy Monday morning to inquire about the progress of the fort. As soon as he walked into my room, I asked him about his weekend. He lowered his eyes and – after a lengthy silence – finally mumbled that his father had bought him a set of tools, and then went off to play golf!

Instantly, I felt a sickening knot in my stomach. I was equally devastated by what had transpired because I had set up this boy for another terrible disappointment. His father had promised me he would work with Timmy. He let us both down. This man seemed totally unconcerned that the boy wanted time with him, not tools. I lost track of Timmy, but there's one thing I do realize now: If a child can't get your attention one way, he'll often seek it in another, less desirable way.

Ramon

Ramon was a foster child who lived in a nearby group home and entered my class halfway through the school year. I met with his caseworker in order to acquire some basic information about him since his permanent records hadn't arrived from his home school.

As we were discussing Ramon's educational program, his caseworker inadvertently passed along startling confidential information. Assuming I already knew about this boy's criminal record, he alluded to Ramon being a convicted rapist who had used a knife to terrorize his victim. Belatedly realizing by my look of alarm that I had had no prior knowledge of this fact, he cautioned me not to tell anyone else as it would be violating this boy's rights and laying the groundwork for my own liability.

I vehemently protested, "What about the rights of our young women? They have a right to a safe environment, don't they?"

Sidestepping that issue, he merely warned me again to keep this information to myself.

Not willing to drop this matter so easily, I asked, "Do you have any daughters?"

"Two," he replied. "Why do you ask?"

"Well, if this kid grabs one of your girls, then you can talk to me about this boy's rights!"

I voiced my concerns about Ramon to the superintendent, and he basically reiterated the advice of the caseworker. Searching for any recourse to protect my female students, I asked him if I could at least make the kid empty his pockets every day before entering my class. That request also produced a negative response. Feeling totally helpless, I vented the rest of my frustration formulating a plan to safeguard my other students.

The next day in class, I concocted some ridiculous story as to why we had to change our present seating arrangement. The only safety precaution I could come up with was to situate Ramon at a desk surrounded by my four toughest boys and to move the girls to the back of the room. I privately told the boy who sat behind Ramon I thought this new kid had some strange habits and asked him to help me keep an eye on him. I guess I could have been setting myself up for a possible lawsuit, but I didn't know what other *unoffending* strategy to devise. While this boy was in my room, I never took my eyes off of him for one moment. Since I wasn't even allowed to tell my co-workers, I was always concerned about his movements when he was out of my sight.

Three weeks later, two police officers entered my room and quickly surveyed the class. Spotting Ramon, they instantly handcuffed him and escorted him to an awaiting squad car. Later that day, I learned they had frisked him after leaving my classroom and had removed a switchblade knife from his possession.

Ramon was arrested for the attempted rape of one of our sophomore girls behind a local business. This young woman just happened to be in my homeroom and talked to me about her terrifying ordeal. Her attacker had grabbed her and held a knife to her throat while also subjecting her to filthy and perverted commentary. At the exact moment he tried to switch the knife to his other hand, she ducked down, broke free of his grasp, and then managed to elude his pursuit. As a result of her testimony, he was convicted a second time, but was out on the streets in less than two years. Astonishingly, our court system had only lightly slapped the hand of a sexual predator.

Connie

Teenage pregnancy presents yet another difficult circumstance for a growing number of secondary students. Following graduation a few years ago, Connie, a particularly delightful student, became pregnant out of wedlock. I found out about this situation from one of her friends whom I asked to inform Connie that I would like to see her.

Again, I had to learn secondhand that she couldn't face me because she thought I would be terribly disappointed in her. In truth, the only disappointment I felt stemmed from her belief that displeasure would be my only reaction.

I finally decided to call Connie at home. I reassured her that her condition didn't change anything between us and that I was there to support her in any way possible. She sounded relieved, and, before ending our rather emotional conversation, promised to come to school the next day.

When she arrived the following morning, we talked privately for a few minutes about her future plans and the dreams that had to be temporarily thrust aside. Then, noting the concern that must have registered on my face, she smilingly reversed our roles by hugging *me* and saying, "Don't worry; we'll get through this!"

Perhaps Connie's words of wisdom encompass the most relevant advice that a veteran teacher can pass on to a newcomer. No matter what unusual and unexpected teaching-related incidents are encountered, they are surmountable. The personal examples I have related from my own career are not meant to discourage anyone from entering the field of education, but simply to forewarn young educators that they will face many more challenges than just the ordinary everyday dissemination of facts and figures to their students. These "extracurricular" experiences need not detract from the incredible enjoyment waiting to be derived from this rewarding profession. Indeed, they might even enhance it!

Most teachers – regardless of the number of years spent in education – suffer from "bouts of doubt." The burning desire to teach on occasion almost gets extinguished. The once fiery enthusiasm is dampened and reduced to a smoldering pile of embers. Yet just when you think there is no fuel left to burn, the *unpredictability factor* can work in your favor. A recent graduate, who studied English as a *third* language, sent me the following heartfelt letter. Obviously composed with great difficulty, it arrived at a time when I most needed it.

Dear Mr. Riffle,

This is _____. Its being a while to me since the last time I saw the smile of your face I hope everything is being better since that time. About me its being much better than it was before I still kept going with my job, also now I got to school the name of the is _____ the is very kool people over there are very nice and helpful to make us to succeed. This I letter I write is most likely a thank you letter or I would say a way to express my feeling how much im greatful to God that you were my teacher. You have helped me to succeed and also to believe in me I want to thank you for all those because with out you I do not know where I would be now cause in only God knows I want to thank you for help me on everything to kept my grade always up and the most import thing is when I was in trouble my mistake fight that I had in school you were 100% by my side and also believe I did not started it first which is the truth I did not started and I want you know to the bottom of my heart I really appreciate for everything you did for me I would never forget you for that.

Sincerely _____

No longer could I remain dispirited. My soul was stoked, and the fire burned brightly again.

The Riffle boys in 1949. Paul was seven and I was three.

In third grade at the Adamstown Elementary School, 1954.

Cocalico Union High School, 1960. Note the phony smile.

As a senior at Kutztown State College, 1968.

My wonderful children (standing) Becky, Matt, (seated) Luke, and Abby.

Mother enjoying the company of her three great-granddaughters: Taylor (behind the chair), Kayla (left), and Mother holding Isabella.

Paul F. Grebinger, my fifth and sixth-grade teacher at the Adamstown Elementary School, was a phenomenal teacher who inspired many of his former students to follow in his footsteps.

My brother Paul with his Iowa farmhands. Without his help and guidance, my teaching career would never have taken place.

Receiving the 2005 Pennsylvania V.F.W. State Teacher of the Year Award from State Commander John Brenner. John was selected as a National All-American Commander by the V.F.W.

Receiving the 2005 V.F.W. National Teacher of the Year Award from V.F.W. National Commander-in-Chief John Furgess and National Ladies Auxiliary President JoAnne Ott.

Conversing with Oprah after being selected as a 2000 Disney American Teacher Award Honoree.

Dr. Constance P. Dent, a former college professor, mentor, and now – more importantly – a friend for life.

Timmy, a truly remarkable young man, in his Ranger uniform.

Sharing another Bulldog victory with Brian. Certain kids become like another member of your family; Brian was one of those kids.

Mindy wearing a Dallas Cowboy shirt just to aggravate me.

Team-teaching with Pauper Boy.

Fred, our room's deer skull psychologist – a great listener, but a poor conversationalist!

Following the terrorist attack on 9/11, Harry was moved to create his drawing entitled "A Nation Remembers."

Harry and I in the classroom. Not only was he the first member of his family to graduate from high school, he was also the first to graduate from college!

I commissioned Harry to create these two sketches. Which one do you think represents the outstanding teacher?

Elaine with our guys (left to right) Paul, Jeremy, Eric, Jeff, Edward, and Peter in the foreground.

Peter is an inspiration to all of us.

A few of my girls clowning around during the photo shoot. Top row (left) Kara, Cortney, Kim, and Rochelle. Bottom row (left) Jennifer, Meg (Notice her hospital ID bracelet), and Mary.

Paul (left) and Eric, two outstanding young artists.

Edward (left) with his Most Improved Academic Student Award and Jeff (right) with his "Medal of Honor"

Getting ready to "duke it out" with Fighting Ron.

Josh, a former student, now a technology assistant, helping Shane with a project.

Eric's signature rose.

Paul's beautiful rendition of a unicorn.

CHAPTER 6

"Misunderstood!"

... Sean

Numerous times throughout this book I have stated or implied that you learn more from your students than they ever learn from you. One of the most eye-opening events to support this claim took place in November of 2001 after Dr. Gerald Achenbach, who wrote the foreword for this book, spoke to me about assisting a doctoral candidate at a Philadelphia university. My surprised reaction had been to teasingly, yet somewhat seriously, ask him if he was sure he wanted me to help someone with a dissertation!

The candidate, Dion Betts, contacted me and asked if he and I could meet with a few of my former students. The purpose of this gathering was simply to interview these adults and ask them to reflect on their experiences in special education classes. Eighteen former students, ranging in age from nineteen to forty-six, agreed to meet with us. To accommodate their schedules, the group was split into two workshops of nine each and met on separate evenings. No one, including myself, was ready for what was about to take place.

The educational process of evaluating students to determine if they should receive special education services is all too familiar: When the test results are in and students are found to be in need of services, meetings are held with the children and their parents. At these meetings the families are assured that these new programs will be what's best for their children. Papers are signed, new schedules are developed, and all involved go about their business. Appropriate plans are put into effect, and we, as educators, feel good about what has been done to help these students.

Let me tell you what has *really* been accomplished: Unwittingly, we have labeled these children for life and have turned their entire world upside down! People in the field of special education rarely stop to think about the emotional and social impact this "Sped" stamp has on kids. The following stories were related to us at the two meetings we convened.

Cortney, a twenty-year-old college student, vividly remembered her introduction to special education classes. She was in third grade where she had a large group of friends and an active social calendar. She explained how common it was to attend numerous birthday parties, sleepovers, and summertime pool parties. Shortly after being placed in a learning support class, these activities came to a halt. She couldn't understand why all of her friends shunned her. Cortney painfully related how she spent many tearful nights in her bedroom, ashamed of whom she had become.

It is very difficult for an eight-year-old child to comprehend why her "best friends" no longer want her around. No doubt about it: Kids can be cruel; anyone who seems different will be ostracized. Unfortunately, Cortney found out the hard way.

Next, she focused on the embarrassment of riding in the "little yellow bus." Probably most school districts in North America own a fleet of yellow vans used to transport small groups of students. Frequently they move our special needs youngsters to their assigned buildings. These vehicles were insignificant to me until one day when I was on bus duty outside the high school. A few of our gifted kids were waiting for a van to take them to a meeting. As the vehicle approached them, one boy turned and said, "Look, we get to ride in a spedmobile!" After hearing this statement, I realized that these vans were just another part of the special education stigma.

I started to take an informal survey of some regular education students. When asked about the purpose of our school's vans, the usual response was, "Oh, they transport the special ed. kids." When I discussed this finding with my students, they all said how they loathed riding in those vehicles. One boy walked more than two miles to school each day in any kind of weather just so he could avoid the dreaded van ride. This is an example of just one more subculture that exists inside every school. The kids know the situation, but we adults rarely do. I'd seen my special needs kids ride those vans for years and never gave it a second thought, but they certainly did.

A few years ago, the son of a close family friend was evaluated, and it was determined he would need special education services when he entered tenth grade. The boy's mother had mentioned periodically throughout his earlier years in school that she was concerned about her son's progress. The day of the meeting was one I'll never forget. I felt uneasy going into the session because of my personal ties with the family, but I also thought they might be more relaxed in dealing with me rather than a staff member they didn't know.

The meeting was heart-wrenching, to say the least. Parents have many of their dreams shattered when the special ed. label is applied to their child. These parents had the look of doom on their faces. I remember thinking that the boy's mother had the same expression on her face as when her mother had died a few years before. I continually tried to reassure them that everything would be fine and that their son would be able to succeed in my classes. On the way out of the meeting, the father asked me through tear-filled eyes if I thought his son would still keep his friends. I responded that being in my classes would have no bearing on his son's social group. Fortunately, in this case I was right.

The process of labeling a child has its innocent inception in grade school. Elementary school reading groups are a prime example. There are *Redbirds*, *Bluebirds*, and *Yellowbirds*. A sports-minded teacher might call the groups *Phillies*, *Yankees*, or *Braves*. It doesn't really matter what the groups are named; everyone knows which group is the least capable. Despite the teacher's attempt to disguise the reading levels, everyone recognizes the "pecking" or "batting" orders.

Sean distinctly remembered the humiliating circumstance he encountered in fourth grade where his teacher had created a step-by-step reading program. As each student successfully completed one of the segments, a cutout star was placed on the wall next to that person's name. Sean told us everyone else in his class had twenty or more stars – he had only two!

Every day when he walked into the classroom, he was unavoidably confronted by that wall and his two reading stars – silent, but glaring, reminders of his failure to perform as well as his classmates. All the other kids were making measurable progress while he had his self-esteem immeasurably damaged. Now a twenty-seven year-old man, he still cannot understand why a teacher would allow him to be mortified in front of everyone.

Honestly, I couldn't explain it myself. The teacher had to see what was happening. It would have been unfair to the other students to disband what I'm sure was a good program – but what about Sean? The teacher could have devised a separate rating system for Sean to allow him to enjoy success at his own pace. His criteria would not have been made public. Instead, only he and the teacher would have been privy to his individualized goals.

I'm not saying every school classroom must become a utopia. As idealistic as that might be, it isn't realistic. The old saying that "life isn't fair" holds true in our schools, too. What I'm actually suggesting is that all teachers must be constantly aware of the strengths and weaknesses of their students, that all try to develop motivational units for kids to compete with themselves – not against their fellow classmates. The Riffle Raider Program (Chapter 4) is an example of this philosophy.

The special education designation has plagued many of my former students throughout their lives. Moreover, this label just doesn't peel off after graduation; it adheres to them as they enter the job market, attempt higher education, and pursue personal relationships. Teachers rarely consider this stigma, but the people assembled in these two meetings made abundantly clear that their lives were negatively impacted, even after receiving their diplomas.

Admittedly, I too, never thought about their special education classification having an adverse effect on dating. My belief had always been that if you have an emotional bond with someone, his/her academic school record shouldn't be a decisive factor in the relationship. Well, maybe it shouldn't matter, but to some people it does. When this subject was first broached, I thought this negative reaction was uncommon, but quickly realized that such was not the case.

All of these former students had much to say on how to handle this sensitive issue, although generally just two attitudes prevailed: The one train of thought was to acknowledge this reality early in a relationship. The second approach was to keep it hidden and hope and pray that no one would ever divulge the "shameful secret." To some partners this information was insignificant, while others received the "I just want to be friends" phone call.

Two of the young women in attendance told me very dissimilar stories about confessing their past to their fiancés. Both of these women perceived sharing their educational "inadequacies" as very risky because both of their fiancés were college graduates.

Kim told us she could no longer keep her secret and sat down with her husband-to-be and confided she had been in special education classes. He took her in his arms and said, "I love you for who you are, and I don't care what classes you took in high school." They have been happily married for more than thirteen years.

Donna's story, unfortunately, did not have the same happy ending. When she told her husband about her educational background, their entire relationship began to unravel. During disagreements, he frequently threw the "sped" label in her face. It was of little consequence to him that she had earned an associate degree as a paralegal; it mattered only that she had been in my classes. He started to talk down to her as if she were a child. Not surprisingly, their marriage lasted a mere four years. One of his parting shots at the divorce hearing made reference to her classification in school. *When we label children as different, that label can brand them forever.*

Lack of common sense by teachers and administrators sometimes astounds me. We all have college degrees, but that doesn't guarantee expertise in compassion. There have been numerous situations when professionals "couldn't see the forest for the trees."

During our meetings, two very conspicuous examples were discussed. Before I relate these circumstances, let me say that our district does everything possible to give all of our students the best education possible. Despite that dedication, some mistakes are inevitable

Jason, age 27, a foreman for an electrical contractor, asked me if I had ever seen his junior high school yearbook. I thought that was an odd inquiry, but it soon made perfect sense. He proceeded to tell us that the class group pictures were all done by homeroom, except for the special education students. They had *Special Education* written under their picture! Jason assured us that he always knew when it was picture day and purposely stayed home.

I personally recalled a similar labeling incident. Two years ago, our district had begun expanding by leaps and bounds, like so many other suburban schools. To my dismay, while touring one of our new elementary schools, I saw a permanent sign outside of a room that proclaimed in bold, black letters: Special Education. I immediately went to the building principal and expressed my displeasure about that sign. She promised me it would be removed. Two months later while attending a staff meeting in that building, I noticed that the sign was still there. Angered, I literally took this situation into my own hands, and the sign came down. The engineering firm that had constructed the school had placed those signs. It wasn't the company's job to know our youngsters, but it certainly was ours. Why the building special education teacher didn't remove that sign is still a mystery to me.

During one of our meetings with Dion, the doctoral candidate, Sean expressed his feelings about being put into special education classes:

"All my life I have felt inferior to everyone else because I couldn't read. I figured I must be really stupid, or I would be able to read. I particularly remember one day in junior high when a substitute teacher asked me to read aloud in class. I couldn't do it and felt so ashamed of myself.

"Throughout my years in school, it was one frustrating, embarrassing moment after another. I thought about quitting, but then what would I do without a high school diploma? So I kept on trying.

"When I was sixteen, I went to a local restaurant and got a job as a busboy. I've worked there for eleven years, and I'm now the assistant manager and head cook.

"I think the proudest moment of my life was when I bought my own home two years ago. It's a small single ranch home, but it's mine, and I'm proud of it. I still can't read very well, but I'm hanging in there."

The pride that registered on Sean's face as he finished speaking radiated to all of us and encouraged others to speak about the special ed. specter that haunted their own lives. Jason readily volunteered to tell his own short academic history: After his career technology teacher had told him that he wasn't smart enough to complete his career center program, Jason successfully pleaded with the instructor to give him a chance and eventually proved he could do it.

When Donna was in school, she had enrolled in a fashion design class at career tech. Her instructor noticed her constant spelling mistakes and called our guidance counselor who informed her that Donna was a special needs student. Donna's teacher had her removed from class because "a special education kid can't do my work." In those days I had no power to keep her in that class. Donna has always said that all she wanted was a fair chance, but didn't get it.

Crystal is another example of a student sidestepping a disability and becoming successful in life. Following high school, she went to work in a retail store as many young people do. She said her hourly rate was okay, but she wanted a more challenging career. She now works for an armored car company in the accounting department. The firm trained her on the job, and this successful experience has given her a strong feeling of self-worth.

At the meetings, I shared my own background that was similar to Jason's. The second semester of my freshman year in college my advisor called me into her office. She told me I wasn't college material and that I should quit school and join the army! I was devastated and also furious that the person who was supposed to help me had such a negative attitude. Fortunately for me, my brother Paul, a junior at Kutztown, stepped in and had me assigned to another advisor.

Incidentally, there was an ironic outcome to that situation. Seeking a summer job following graduation, I was one of three people selected to run our local Operation Head Start, which at that time was a nine-week summer program. Incredibly, one applicant for a teaching position was my former advisor. While I went over her application and read her excellent resume, she looked like someone sitting in the electric chair just before the switch was thrown! When the interview was over and she rose to leave my office, I couldn't help but add, "As you can see, I did graduate from college." In spite of my personal feelings, I hired her anyway believing she had the best qualifications for the job.

The role of the teacher in helping a child develop a positive self-image can never be overemphasized. In my opinion, however, the most important people are the child's parents. I can usually tell the type of home environment a child comes from without actually knowing the family. Children who come from dysfunctional families frequently drag their emotional baggage to school.

During the course of the meeting, Ben told us about his home circumstances and how his own father had marked him for life. Ben had a severe disability in reading and constantly struggled to improve these skills. His father was verbally abusive. He ridiculed Ben and referred to him as "Gomer Pyle." When he was only fifteen, Ben set a goal for himself: On his eighteenth birthday he would move out of the house. The day he turned eighteen was the last day he lived in his home. He is now twenty-eight and has no contact with his father.

Sadly, stories like Ben's are too numerous to recount. This parent missed the priceless opportunity to share a lifetime with a great young man. I don't know if it's embarrassment or if it's shame that drives these parents to mistreat their own children. Possibly they had dreams of their children being cheerleaders or captains of the football team and couldn't get past this disappointment.

During both of these meetings the kids and I discussed how we developed techniques to help us disguise our disabilities. We all agreed that writing, especially spelling, has been a challenge for us. We constantly search for words we know how to spell when writing. This is a very common problem facing learning- disabled people. A couple of the college kids said they would be lost without the spellcheck feature on their computers.

Pronunciation of words has always been a source of embarrassment for me. I thought it was just a personal reaction until these meetings were held. Rochelle told us how she often struggled with this problem at her part-time job. She explained that she worked at a ski shop where many of the items sold are from foreign countries – a double whammy! Being told by her employer to pick up a certain brand name highlighted her reading disability, and being asked by a customer what brand it was presented a pronunciation problem. Both difficulties are reading-related and both can humiliate a learning- disabled person.

One point everyone strongly agreed upon was that people – friends, relatives, teachers, peer group – look at you and treat you in a different manner after you are labeled as learning-disabled. Sad recollections such as Meganne's should never have to be repeated: "I wanted my mom to sign me out of school when I was in junior high because it got so bad. I'm a real person even though I have to sit down in a wheelchair all the time; I'm still a real person even if I'm learning-disabled. I can still be useful. People treat us as if our learning disability is a disease they can catch!" Truly, educators have to be sensitive to this issue and eliminate this harmful reaction whenever possible.

All young people face various problems when growing up; feeling inferior intellectually to your peer group is especially upsetting. All my life, and even now, I have been envious of highly intelligent people. As ridiculous as it sounds, I have felt that intelligent people have fewer problems than people like me. This may be a foolish way of thinking, but I was surprised to find out that my former students felt the same way.

Jeremy, who is dyslexic, said, "Regular education teachers don't know how to deal with us. As soon as they know we are disabled learners, they think we don't want to learn and that we're just plain lazy. The worst part is that they treat us that way." That statement struck a nerve in me, and I told the group that I wish I had a dollar for every time I had been told that exact thing. Also knowing that former athletes whom I've taught were treated differently by the coaches when they found out these players were "Riffle's kids," I made sure – whenever possible – coaches never knew when they were dealing with my students.

Paul recounted his experiences in relationships with his regular education friends: "Whenever the subject of who had which teacher came up, I would pretend I was in regular classes and have the names of those teachers memorized." Paul was an outstanding artist (his unicorn drawing is displayed in this book), but he was ashamed to tell his friends about his disability.

These feelings of rejection and isolation were a common denominator for many of these former students. Donna informed us it was a regular occurrence for her special ed. group to be spit upon by "normal" students passing them in the hallway or on the stairs. And although not all reactions were this extreme, not even one child should have to suffer any of these indignities due to "advertising" their mental or physical limitations.

Besides the labeling stigma, Sean pointed out another unaddressed area. He simply stated that we all learn in different ways, and teachers should remember that. He recalled how one of his former elementary teachers basically used the same method to teach every subject. This method relied heavily on reading comprehension skills. Since Sean was an auditory learner, he was at a huge disadvantage compared to the better readers in his class.

Unfortunately, Donna knew firsthand what could happen when a child is left behind literally and figuratively because one method of learning isn't sufficient. Failing to achieve the same success as her sixth-grade classmates while working on a social studies unit, Donna was made to stay inside and watch from the window as the other kids excitedly lined up and vied to be first to break open a piñata, the culminating event of the unit. So many years later, the hurt and bewilderment over not being allowed to participate in this much-anticipated event were still evident on her face and in her voice. Donna suggested that books should be put on tape to help auditory learners. This recommendation met with unanimous approval by the rest of the group.

Elementary teachers need to be especially aware of their students' learning difficulties so problems can be identified, diagnosed, and treated at an earlier age. Mary related how she had been passed on in grades 1, 2, and 3 despite being unable to read. Her parents were simply told that she was retarded. Fortunately, after the discovery of an undiagnosed learning disability, Mary finally began to experience success in her later school years.

Sean explained that his special education teachers used various techniques to teach each lesson. He felt that these teachers seemed to be more patient and understood the concept that people learn in different ways. I couldn't make a blanket statement concerning Sean's observation, but one explanation might be that special education teachers know and expect their students will need different teaching methods. Regular education teachers often have not been trained to deal with learning-disabled students and never have given much thought to these students mixed in with their nondisabled students. This deficiency must be addressed in college courses that educate our future teachers.

Dion eventually asked both groups if their special needs programs were an asset or a hindrance. Despite the misgivings they had voiced, all the people thought it was a major help. Four or five agreed that they would never have graduated without our assistance. Jason pointed out that a tremendous strength of most special education teachers is making kids believe in themselves. Tiffany echoed the same feeling about needing someone to believe in her as all other heads were nodding in agreement.

When people asked me about goals for my kids, I said that evening, "When my kids look in the mirror, I want them to like what they see. I want to make them believe in themselves." It's not that I won't tell students when they are wrong, but – more importantly – that I will tell them when they are right. My students have told me this affirmation is what made them feel special and more self-assured. Encouraging students to believe in themselves provides them with the confidence needed to go forward and not let past failures and misconceptions about their intelligence interfere with achieving worthy goals. Encouragement is perhaps the most important concept that teachers can embrace.

Following each meeting, everyone was physically and emotionally drained. These former students shed many tears as they dredged up painful memories and expressed lingering resentments. Psychological scars, thought to be healed, became raw, exposed wounds again. We became misty-eyed listeners as these testimonials unveiled some of the more subtle inadequacies of the special education program.

Despite this attempt, the stories they related and the emotional cleansing that took place could never be adequately described. The passion and sadness displayed by these young men and women instilled in me a revived empathy for what they had once experienced and what they still endure as a result of their earlier placements in school. Once again, my students taught me more than I could ever know on my own. I am indebted to them for sharing their thoughts, observations, and opinions. With bittersweet insight, I realized that I could have been a better teacher if I had known then what I know now. At this point I could not erase the past for these students, but the outcome of these meetings could be used to effect positive changes for future special education students.

While ending the second session, Dion asked the assembled group what they thought would be a good title for his dissertation. Instantly Sean called out, "Misunderstood!" All of us in attendance immediately *understood* and agreed whole-heartedly with his suggestion.

CHAPTER 7

I will always blame myself.

...Vickie

Not long after the two meetings with our candid graduates had concluded, we began to entertain the idea of inviting parents of former students to a third meeting. For any improvements in the educational process to occur, it would be equally important to have the parents of learning-disabled students relate their stories and voice their opinions. We decided it was worth a try and soon extended invitations to several parents.

The response was very rewarding. Most of the parents who agreed to attend were the mothers and fathers of the young people who had participated in the two earlier meetings. Our hope was that these people, like their children, would freely express their deepest concerns to us. We were not disappointed by what transpired that evening. They were ready – and just as willing – to share their own tribulations during the tumultuous journey their children had taken through the educational system.

The meeting began in an upbeat manner as we joked about trivial topics such as the demise of Mindys' parent's lowly Dallas Cowboys. But after we were at ease with each other, light-hearted banter was soon replaced by more serious dialogue. To begin the session, the parents were asked to introduce themselves and state the name(s) and age(s) of their children. Quickly we determined that their progeny ranged in age from twenty to thirty-one, and that all were classified as either learning-disabled, emotionally disturbed, or brain-injured.

Prior to the meeting, we had developed a set of questions that paralleled the topics discussed by their children. How similar would their answers be to the ones expressed at our previous meetings? Would their responses be vastly different? Regardless of their content, the parental viewpoints would undoubtedly offer intimate and invaluable insight into the world of learning-disabled children.

The first question posed to this group was *"Did any of you have trouble learning as a child?"* To initiate the discussion, I voluntarily commented on the various academic problems I had encountered as a student in the 60s. I explained the three levels of education in existence at that time: college preparatory, general, and mentally retarded. All students had to fit into one of these categories. I briefed the parents about my incessant struggle to maintain passing grades, how teachers constantly ridiculed me for being lazy and not taking school seriously, and then frankly admitted that what had saved me from failing were projects, speeches, and reports my mother had edited.

Many parents confessed they had also experienced learning difficulties. Vickie, who is a registered nurse, told us that she still panics when confronted with math problems. Two other parents also commented on how math was their "Waterloo." Cindy said she has a sequencing impediment, which she referred to as a "visual perception" problem. I agreed that some kids' disabilities probably are caused by abnormal visual perceptions, and I had a personal reason for endorsing this theory.

When my son Luke experienced some reading difficulty in elementary school, our school psychologist suggested *vision therapy*. This man is an outstanding psychologist, and I valued his opinion. He cautioned me that some professionals were critical of this "smoke and mirrors" method that produced very few, if any, measurable results. A personal friend of mine happened to be a nationally recognized ophthalmologist. When I discussed vision therapy with him, he told me I might as well build a bonfire with my money because this type of therapy was useless. Perplexed about what course of action to pursue, I nevertheless thought that if this could help my son in any way, it was worth the cost.

Luke underwent therapy for twelve months, and it seemed to work wonders for him. Does this successful outcome prove that this type of treatment works? Not really. One case is certainly not a scientific study. Would his reading have improved without this type of help? No one knows for sure, but it convinced me that vision therapy was at least one viable strategy to assist poor readers.

The next question presented to the parents was *"Did you think your child had a disability before the school contacted you for testing?"* Vickie told us that her youngest child had some physical abnormalities as a newborn. Since their daughter had these obvious physical problems, she and her husband were also concerned about possible mental deficiencies. This child was diagnosed as learning-disabled at an early age while the older sibling's learning problem went undetected until he was in seventh grade. Vickie said the positive results of her daughter's tests prompted her to request an evaluation for her son as well. Otherwise, his learning disability might have gone unnoticed for an even longer period of time

Dotty commented on her son's behavior as a preschooler. She informed us there are three children in their family, the two oldest being girls. The two daughters excelled in the classroom, constantly read books, and had a real interest in school. The mother lamented that she couldn't get through even short children's books without her son's losing interest. When she quizzed her child on what she had just read, he showed very little comprehension. Pat, the boy's father, said, "At the time, we thought it was because he was a boy and the baby of the family!"

Both of their daughters graduated from local universities. Surprisingly, the oldest daughter was diagnosed with a disability her senior year in college. The parents explained how Cori had to read things three or four times before the material "sank in." She never realized she had a disability, but instead thought everyone had to read things repeatedly. Indeed, there are many people with disabilities who don't realize they have a problem because they have learned to compensate. They have developed coping methods throughout their lives and are unaware that not everyone learns the way they do.

One parent discussed how their son seemed to have unlimited amounts of energy – so much that he couldn't control his movements. In elementary school, he was constantly disciplined for not being able to sit still in class. The punishment the teacher deemed appropriate was to have him remain at his desk and miss recess. Here was a child with a nuclear power plant of energy, and he was made to miss playtime as a corrective measure!

The parents finally convinced the teacher that keeping him in his seat as a punishment wasn't a good idea. In fact, considering the extent of his hyperactivity, I'm sure the teacher was penalized also! Finally the young man was diagnosed with a disability while in second grade. During his initial IEP meeting, suggestions were made by the team that helped him significantly.

Next, the parents were asked to describe their reactions when told their children had disabilities. Janet told us about her oldest daughter Rochelle's initial I.E.P. meeting. She and her husband were called in to confer with the principal and the school's psychologist to discuss the ER (educational report). As the meeting progressed, she and her husband were grilled about the possibility of having physically abused their daughter. Exasperated, they were also asked if they were drug users!

Devastated by these questions, Janet invited her uncle, who has his Ph.D. and works for a New York State school district, to attend the next meeting. That meeting concluded abruptly when Janet was told that her daughter would never be capable of anything more challenging than flipping burgers at a fast food restaurant. She went home and told her husband that as soon as it was financially feasible, they were moving to our school district.

Rochelle entered my classroom when she was in tenth grade. I knew only that she was Janet's child. I had known Janet and her two sisters when they were students in our high school, but I was totally unaware of her daughter's educational background. I taught Rochelle for three years and found her to be a well- organized, mature, motivated, and above-average student.

I remember in particular her keen interest in my disability. She quizzed me frequently on how I managed to graduate from college with a disability. I told her that I had had a lifelong dream of becoming a teacher, and that I wouldn't let anything stand in my way. She asked me if I thought she could be successful in college. I responded in a positive manner, telling her that if she worked very hard, I thought she could do it. I cautioned her, as I do all students who ask me that question: *College is an opportunity for more education. It's not the beginning, nor is it the end of your life. Go there, do your very best, and see what you can make happen. If you're not successful there, you'll find another occupation that is right for you.* I'm proud to say that Rochelle is attending a state university where she is a junior majoring in special education. The only burgers she plans to flip are on her backyard grill!

Most of the parents in attendance said their children had been identified before reaching fourth grade. It was disturbing to learn, however, that three of the parents had children who weren't identified until junior high school. I told the parents that these older children seem to be the ones who encounter the most problems in school. Apparently the earlier a child is diagnosed, the easier the transition is into learning support classes. Only one child was identified as late as tenth grade.

This latecomer was Janet's youngest daughter Jessica. Janet said that she was running with a "rough crowd" and was a problem both at home and in school. School administrators were looking for alternative placement for her. All the while Janet kept asking them if they thought it was possible that Jessica had a learning disability. School officials told her the issue was discipline – not a learning disability.

Finally, just before entering tenth grade, Jessica was found to have a specific learning disability. Coincidentally, she was enrolled in a summer school class at our high school. One day I happened to see Janet in the hallway as she was waiting to pick up Jessica after class. During this chance encounter, I found out her daughter had been recently identified. I asked Janet's permission to talk to Jessica. She pleaded for me to do so as soon as possible since Jessica was planning to quit school.

The next day I went to school with the sole purpose of finding Jessica. After we were seated in an empty classroom, I began the rather one-sided conversation:

"Do you know who I am?"

She curtly said, "Yes, I know who you are."

By her attitude I could tell she was "thrilled" to see me! The more I talked to her, the more she tuned me out. Finally, I used a question technique that I've used for years with kids in similar situations: "Do you want to be where your friends are going to be in ten years?"

She hesitated, so I patiently repeated the question.

Sheepishly, she said, "No."

"Then," I told her, "now is the time to snap your life around and to begin applying yourself in school!"

She replied, "I'm quitting school anyway, so what does it matter?"

I refrained from going into the *without-a-high-school-diploma* speech, which she had already heard too often. Instead, since she was still too young to withdraw herself from school, I asked her to consider the following suggestion: "You give me just three weeks of your full effort, and I'll give back to you the same amount of my effort. If, after that time period, you feel I'm wasting your time and you still want to withdraw, then do it. If not, and you want to try another three weeks, we'll take it from there."

And so Jessica and I began our roller-coaster relationship. For three weeks she gave me her best effort and scored extremely well on all material taught to her. Little did she know that I had orchestrated all of her courses so she would experience success and continue in school. I called her aside after the initial three weeks and asked her if she wanted to quit or try to endure another three weeks. Acting as though the question exasperated her, she responded, "I'll try *just* three more weeks."

Her nonchalant attitude didn't fool me. As I had watched her saunter away, my first thought had been *No, Jess, you are hooked on success, and you and I both know it, although I realize your pride will never let you admit that fact.* Off and on throughout the next two years, she'd threaten to quit just to "crank me up."

Janet told me that the first year I had Jess in class, she frequently complained to her about the annoying Mr. Riffle. "He drives me crazy! Every time he sees me in the hall he calls my name. He drives me nuts! Why does he do that?" Janet laughed and later informed her husband that I was watching everything their daughter was doing unbeknownst to her. Janet also told the group that on several occasions I was at her home when Jess returned. She'd see me, ditch the cigarette, and ask me why I was there bothering her, at the same time sitting down next to me to talk.

I don't want anyone to assume that our relationship was all "smooth sailing." It wasn't. One month she was amicable, and the next month I couldn't say or do anything right. In spite of everything, I *never* gave up on her. During her senior year, she was on the honor roll every quarter. No one was prouder of her at graduation than I was. Following the ceremony, we embraced and shed tears of joy. Jess is now enrolled in college majoring in web page design.

Pat and Dotty continued their reflections on the problems their son had encountered throughout elementary school, describing one failure after another. Prior to one test, Dotty and her son had spent a total of five hours studying the material. He knew the facts cold but still failed the test. Dumbfounded, she sat him down and quizzed him on the subject matter again, and he knew it all. Dotty was completely frustrated and couldn't understand why he had failed.

This mother recalled that one weekend in elementary school, he had had twenty-four papers to complete. When Dotty called the teacher to ask why he had so much work to do, the teacher responded that he couldn't complete his work on time like the other kids. She hadn't wanted to upset him by forcing him do it, so she had sent the assignments home. The teacher's explanation didn't stop there: She added that Dotty's son didn't want to learn, was disruptive, and definitely did not want to be in school. At the time, he was only in first grade! As he progressed through elementary school, persistent discipline problems accompanied his lack of academic success. When he finally entered junior high school, the district was looking for alternative placement for him.

Eventually, their son was diagnosed with a learning disability compounded by emotional issues. An I.E.P. was put into place, and the boy finally achieved some academic success. By the time he was a senior, his name was a constant fixture on the honor roll. During his graduation ceremony, the school presented him with the Most Improved Student Award. With the clarity that only hindsight can provide, it is evident that his entire school experience would probably have been more positive if he had been identified earlier.

Cindy's daughter had been in a wheelchair since early childhood. She had a sweet personality and was adored by all who knew her. However, her calm demeanor soon disappeared when she entered school. Her problems surfaced early in first grade, where she was prone to emotional outbursts and was utterly frustrated with her schoolwork. By the time she reached sixth grade, her problems had escalated until she didn't even want to go to school. She was an angry child and had good reason to be: She was confined to a wheelchair and also couldn't stay abreast of her classmates academically.

Finally, in eighth grade, her daughter was diagnosed with a specific learning disability. When Cindy inquired why she hadn't been identified earlier, the answer stunned her: "She was already given one label; why give her another one?" Naturally, that "label" would have given her more support at an earlier age and a much better chance for success in school.

One of my major concerns has always been the child who "falls through the cracks." Far too many kids go through school without being diagnosed. It would be interesting to know the number of high school dropouts who were unidentified LD kids. These students never received the support necessary to achieve success in school. Cases such as the three just highlighted happen far too often. Why aren't schools taking a closer look at students who are failing?

One possible solution might be fairly easy to implement: requiring all regular education majors to take undergraduate credits in teaching learning-disabled students in mainstreamed classes. Such courses would not only deal with educating the learning-disabled child, but would also help the teacher recognize characteristics to look for in undiagnosed students. If a teacher doesn't know the basic characteristics of learning-disabled children, how are they supposed to pinpoint a child with a possible learning disability?

I teach a summer workshop called *Learning Disabilities: The Unseen Disabilities.* This program is designed for our regular education teachers in grades K-4. I discuss the various characteristics they should look for and adjustments for the LD children in their classrooms. I emphasized K-4 instruction because that is when most kids start receiving special services. As previously discussed, the early-identified child seems to find more success and has a better overall attitude than the child who faces a lonely uphill battle until he or she is labeled in junior high school – if at all.

One of our major concerns at this meeting was discussing the mistakes we've made with kids and how to avoid repeating them. The one complaint that all the parents voiced was one I had never considered: removing children from class in order to receive the "specials." To teachers, this accommodation is just another part of our day, but to the student who is being pulled out of class, it's a major embarrassment. One parent said that elementary kids usually won't say anything about this situation because they're too intimidated by the teacher. However, inwardly little Johnny in first grade is reacting to being yanked from class for his remedial reading program. This very issue *was* frequently discussed at home.

A difficult dilemma that teachers face is how to support these kids without isolating them from their classmates. This problem is very complex and not easily solved. These kids desperately need the special programs, but with the time restraints that are put on everyone, helping these kids without removing them from class is virtually impossible. I don't think there is one solution; instead, I think that each school must address this situation on an individual basis.

The "yellow van" stigma also resurfaced during this meeting. As I listened to the parents discuss how their kids hated riding in these vans, I wondered again how I could have been so "clueless" all these years. I've always prided myself on being in tune with my students and their feelings, but I totally missed the mark on this one. My kids and I periodically sit and talk about the various aspects of our program, and never once did anyone mention the dreaded yellow vans.

Another point emphasized by the parents was that certain teachers don't listen to what parents have to say about their own child. One parent rightfully observed, "We have raised our son since birth, and although we aren't teachers, we know and understand our child. Furthermore, we know what motivates him and what shuts him down. Our opinion should count, but too often it doesn't." Her complaint underscored what I have always believed: *Be a better listener; you'll be surprised what you learn.*

Janet referred again to the story about her daughter's first IEP meeting. Not only was she trying to understand and process all that was happening, she was also trying to decipher acronyms such as NOREP, ER, and IEP while digesting the "fact" that her child wasn't capable of more highly skilled employment. She questioned the validity of that conclusion. *How can these people know what my daughter can or can't do in another twenty years?* Three or four other parents recalled being on the receiving end of similar negative assessments of their children.

Cindy emphasized that teachers should never set boundaries on what they think a child can learn, reaffirming my own philosophy. Teachers sometimes feel they know what is best for a child, but shouldn't erect roadblocks to other possible avenues of exploration. Teachers should guide kids and encourage them, and they should never discourage them. If children have future aspirations that really are beyond their reach, they'll find that out soon enough on their own.

Frequently when discussing goals with students, I use myself as an example. I mention my strong points and my limitations, also stressing that all people have limitations – no matter who they are. Normally, I use a student sitting before me as an example. Harry, who graduated in

2003, was an outstanding artist. To underscore that point, I compared his ability to my notorious lack of artistic talent – his expertly shaded portraits to my stick figures. I never had any delusions about being an artist, but I discovered my limits by myself.

How can teachers or psychologists sit with the parent of a young child and predict the child's future? What would my baseball coaches or teachers have said about my future abilities? As a nine-year-old pitcher, I couldn't find home plate with a map and a compass; as a twenty-year-old, the Atlanta Braves drafted me to play baseball professionally. In school, academic success seemed beyond my reach, and yet through perseverance and hard work, I graduated from college and have now taught for more than thirty-five years. No one knows the future or how a young person may or may not succeed. Only time will reveal that ultimate answer.

Vickie expressed another interesting point that warrants repeating. She said, "If you as a teacher are continually butting heads with a kid, or the kid isn't comprehending what you're teaching, go to someone else and ask for suggestions on a different approach to reach this child. It seems that certain teachers have an ego problem and won't ask anyone for help." Her next words echoed the exact same sentiments of our former students: "Kids learn in different ways, and what works for one child may not work for another one."

That repeated observation should be taken seriously by all educators. Teachers have many students and cannot always be experts on what method works best with each individual. However, they should always be receptive to trying new strategies and motivational techniques. Teachers have three valuable and available human resources: other teachers, the parents, or the child in question.

Mindy's mother cited a perfect example. When her blind daughter was learning to count coins, she was expected to master the concept with paper coins provided by the teacher. Since Mindy couldn't see the coins like the other kids, it was an unending and frustrating struggle for her. Coins are very distinguishable by a blind person just as they are by a sighted person – but in a different manner. The size, thickness, ridges or lack of ridges enable a blind person to tell them apart. Mindy couldn't feel these dissimilarities with paper coins. When Vickie asked the teacher to use actual coins with her daughter, the teacher told her she couldn't do that, although she never gave a legitimate reason why. The mother took it upon herself to teach Mindy at home using real coins. Chances are this teacher had never taught a blind child before and yet ignored a parent's suggestion on how best to help the child.

I commented that when I have a student I can't seem to reach, I make arrangements to meet with that child privately. Such a meeting is not a sure fix, but it does indicate to any student that you sincerely care. You demonstrate not only your willingness to take your time to talk with the student, but more importantly, your desire to listen to her or him. The communication door has been opened, and that is the most important aspect in any relationship. Amazingly, you might discover that the problem you're having in your classroom has absolutely nothing to do with school or you.

For instance, years ago, Norman, who was a sophomore in one of my history classes, just didn't seem able to focus on anything I taught. He wasn't a troublemaker; he just seemed lethargic in class. We met privately, and even then he had difficulty focusing on our conversation. I finally got to the root of his problem: food, or, more precisely, the lack of it. The only meal Norman received every day was his school lunch. He never had breakfast and rarely a cooked supper. From that moment on, he had a daily breakfast: Milk, orange juice, and peanut butter and jelly sandwiches were on his preschool menu. This wasn't exactly eggs Benedict, but it was certainly better than nothing at all. The family was also encouraged to sign up for government food stamps. Norman's lack of concentration came about for one simple reason: He was hungry. Subsequently, his attitude changed and his grades improved. Not only did he have food to eat, but he also realized he was being sustained by caring teachers. His opinion about school changed drastically.

When I asked the parents if any of their kids had ever mentioned my rule on lunch, two of them said, "Mr. Riffle says if you don't have lunch money, you better go to him and get some." Smiling at their mimicked rendition of my standing order, I explained that students could expect a stern lecture from me if I find out they didn't eat lunch because they lacked money. In fact, I stress this point so emphatically that their classmates will "roll over" on them if they don't eat lunch. On numerous occasions I have gone to the cafeteria and rounded up some food for a kid who hasn't eaten that day. The students think I make a big deal out of this only because I don't want them to go hungry. However, the reality goes deeper than that. This is just another way to show my students that I'm concerned about them and care about them as people. This gesture has aided me greatly over the years in classroom management situations. You may or may not get your money back, but the eventual net worth is considerably more enriching than the initial, low-cost investment.

Next, Pat interjected a problem his son had while in school: Certain teachers set up long-range goals for their students that seemed unobtainable for his son. For example, if a teacher assigned a project that was due in a month, his son gave up before he ever started. This type of extended goal overwhelmed his child. Giving the student daily goals as opposed to a month-long goal would have been much more appropriate.

Janet commented that behavioral goals should also be limited in time. She said, "Don't tell students that they will be rewarded for a month of acceptable class behavior. Instead, make it daily – or even less in some cases. Kids need to see that their goals are obtainable within a short time period."

I cautioned the parents that rewards for appropriate behavior must be thought out very carefully. I recalled one situation I had had as a young teacher. My classroom at that time was run like a one-room school. I told a boy who had trouble controlling himself in class that if he could behave, he would be given five minutes of free time for every day that he followed classroom rules. That meant that by Friday he could earn up to twenty-five minutes to sit and relax at the end of the day.

I was very proud of myself because I had created a way to modify his behavior. However, this program lasted for only three weeks because another one of my students questioned my procedures.

"Why is Charles being given free time on Friday afternoons?"

"Charles," I explained, "has trouble controlling himself in class, and this will help him follow the classroom rules."

"What about me?" she asked.

"What about you?" I responded. I wasn't getting her message.

Miffed, she continued, "I do my work and don't give you any grief in class, but I don't get time off. That's not fair."

She was right, of course. I realized then that you couldn't reward kids for reaching behavioral goals with special privileges that the students who followed the rules didn't receive. To rectify this inequity, I extended the free-time goal to all of my kids. There was a benefit from that twenty-five-minute block on Fridays that I hadn't anticipated originally: It provided a time for all of them to discuss issues relevant to their lives and to come to a better understanding of each other. From that time on, I worked these programs in reverse. Children who misbehaved would lose classroom privileges, not gain one that was denied to the other kids already exhibiting good behavior.

When I asked for other suggestions from the group, Craig spoke up. "You people (teachers) work very closely with our kids. It was very helpful when you talked to our son and helped him develop goals for his future." Again, I explained that at times this is very difficult. You can measure a person's I.Q., his or her reading and math levels, but you can't measure motivation.

I related a story my mother, a guidance counselor, had told me many years ago about a set of twin boys who had gone to our school. Their dad had an appointment to see her early one morning to discuss what courses of study she felt his sons should pursue. Mother advised him to enroll both of them in the College Preparatory program. She frankly admitted that it would be a struggle because boys often mature at a slower pace. Those two boys are now grown men with their PhD's in education and are both school administrators. This is not to say that all kids are college material. My point is that motivation will allow some kids to achieve goals that most people would consider impossible for them to obtain.

Vickie broached another concern. She fervently believed that disabled kids should be in classes with "normal" students. She said, "All students should see what these handicapped kids go through every day of their lives. They should see how these students struggle with simple tasks such as tying their shoes or putting on their coats. Empathy and understanding come from interaction, not segregation."

In addition, Mike felt that open dialog between teachers and students is paramount. He commented that when he was in school, teachers seemed to show an indifference towards students and their problems. "No one ever asked me what was wrong when I was upset. I had to work it out on my own." He was glad that his kids had teachers who cared about them as people, not just how well they performed in a classroom. Mike wondered why more regular education teachers don't take a greater personal interest in their students.

I explained that it's not that they don't care; it's a matter of numbers versus time. For example, I will have numerous kids twice, sometimes three times a day in classes that rarely exceed fifteen students. A regular education class will average twenty-five kids per period. Every time the bell rings, twenty-five different students – or more – walk into the room. Those teachers normally don't have the opportunity to interact with the kids as our special education staff does. Time just doesn't permit it.

Cindy mentioned how wonderful our instructional assistants had been when working with her daughter. As the kids would say, "back in the day" no one had assistants in the classroom. Now we couldn't function without them. Teachers need top-flight assistants just as much as the kids do. People outside of the classroom might see these aides as clerical staff. How mistaken they are! In truth, our assistants are invaluable teaching assets. While I'm instructing the whole class, my aide might be working with a child who needs one-on-one help. On test days she will take a selected group of kids to an empty room to facilitate oral test taking. This essential interaction goes on every day in special education classes across the nation.

When the subject of young teachers was raised, one parent mentioned that a new teacher his son had had in elementary school came across as knowing everything about teaching. At a parent conference this teacher talked to the parents as if they were ignorant people. On the way home from the meeting, they had asked themselves a legitimate question: *How could he know so much about teaching in his first year?*

I agreed that sometimes such smugness occurred and also expressed hope that it was a rarity. I reflected back on my days as a laborer at a local steel mill. In May the young engineers hired were issued shiny, new, white hardhats. They'd come down to the hot mill with one of two attitudes: *I'm a college graduate, and I know how to run a steel mill* or *I'm a new employee who doesn't know a thing about the steel business, but would like to learn. Will you teach me?* The second group made it, while the first group rarely lasted the summer. I assured the parents that most young teachers come in with a positive attitude and are open to suggestions from older, more experienced teachers.

Cindy expressed another of her strong beliefs: "Teachers should judge students on their 'face value,' not on their past records. Don't prejudge kids; judge them on their relationship with you." Cindy remembered cringing at a transition meeting when she heard her daughter's teacher tell the receiving teacher that Meganne had real "anger issues." She wondered how this new teacher would treat her child. I agreed that this was a "double-edged sword," because when a discipline issue arises, the parent will have to wonder if it's an actual problem or the result of expectations.

Another mother asked the assembled parents if their children ever blamed them for their disabilities. All but one put their hands up. This question began a major discussion, and it was revealing to examine this common denominator. Equally astounding was the fact that the mothers in attendance blamed themselves for their children's problems. I tried to point out that their sense of guilt is unwarranted, that arguments with adolescents are commonplace in most homes. When a child, especially in the middle of a heated disagreement, blames the parent for his/her disability, it is extremely hurtful. Dotty said that her son has always blamed her for his problem because he felt that his two older sisters received preferential treatment for being good students. The anger that frequently accompanies disabilities can cause major problems within the home. Certainly a common human fault is finding someone to blame rather than accepting the fact that some things just happen.

When the meeting ended, we were all emotionally spent. The unburdening of guilt and blame had taken its toll. However, there was also a shared sense of relief among the parents knowing – even belatedly – that they hadn't been alone in their struggle to raise a learning-disabled child. One parent summed it up with these parting words: "Our kids, no matter what their disability, come home to us every day at three o'clock. Teachers have no idea of the stress we live with every day of our lives. Raising a 'normal' child is stressful enough, but add to it a disability of some type, and it becomes increasingly more difficult."

The cooperation from all of these parents is especially commendable since their children can no longer benefit from any future reforms. The stress in their lives as they gingerly guided their learning-disabled children through their school years and beyond was quite evident. Although many progressive special education programs have been implemented, clearly there is still room for improvement. Administrators, teachers, parents, and students need to listen to each other and work together to provide the best educational environment possible. The messages have been delivered; let's not wait too long for the answers.

CHAPTER 8

"Never give up on any kids; you may be all they have."
...Helen T. Riffle

The impact you have on young people in your role as a teacher is so astronomical that it cannot possibly be measured. To fully grasp what that means, reflect back on your own life. Naturally, parents, relatives, and friends profoundly influenced your personal development. But at some time in your life, there was probably a special teacher who indelibly molded a part of your soul.

The incredible person who fulfilled that role in my life was Mr. Paul Grebinger, instructor of the fifth and sixth grades at the Adamstown Elementary School. He was someone whom I always admired for his enthusiastic approach to teaching. His passion for the outdoors often led us out of the classroom for nature hikes on beautiful fall and spring days. While conducting these walking lectures, he simultaneously piqued and satisfied our natural curiosity by pointing out telltale signs of hidden wildlife and by identifying various types of foliage in the nearby forest.

Even though I was only eleven years old at the time, I knew exactly what I wanted to be when I grew up: a teacher, just like Mr. Grebinger. I'm sure he never realized the tremendous impact he had on my life. Most teachers never consciously analyze the ripple effect of their words and deeds. Therefore, as you teach, it behooves you to remember: *You are at all times a role model for your students; do everything possible to make sure your influence is a positive one.* As my own mother once wisely counseled: *Never give up on any kids because you may be all they have.*

Kitty

A quiet and extremely thin young woman named Kitty was in my homeroom during the 1977-78 school year. Since her desk just happened to be next to mine, it gradually became customary for her to talk to me early every morning. As the days passed by, she began to confide in me about personal family matters. Her parents had divorced a few years before, and each had remarried. As a result, Kitty felt abandoned by both parents and fell prey to an eating disorder, anorexia nervosa.

At that time, I had never heard of this affliction and was totally unaware of the psychological implications that accompanied this prolonged aversion to eating food. I still shudder remembering how I touched her shoulder one day and made unexpected contact with protruding tendons and ligaments. It totally unnerved me that she was 5'8" and weighed only eighty-three pounds! Fortunately, as the year progressed, Kitty appeared less dispirited and more emotionally stable while at the same time adding some desperately needed pounds to her frail frame.

A chance encounter brought us face to face again a few years after she had graduated from high school. She was married and looked wonderful. She told me I had expedited her recovery more than all of the psychiatrists she had ever seen because I truly cared and wasn't making money off her disease. Truthfully, all I did was listen and give her some basic advice.

Teachers are expected to be good speakers when, in fact, they should be even better listeners. Many students need their teachers to sincerely pay attention to what they have to say. Frequently, these kids are dealing with issues that people their age should not have to confront. Talking about nonacademic subjects is not wasting class time; what really transpires is a critical bonding between teacher and students. Indeed, the mastery of subject matter may never even take place if this emotional connection is overlooked or ignored.

Tom

Tom, one of my students in the 1980s, had a mother who had emotionally distanced herself from her son. She provided the basic physical necessities for his survival, but little more. During the Christmas season when he was in tenth grade, the kids in my classroom were discussing among themselves what they hoped to receive for Christmas. I overheard Tom saying that he would not be getting anything. Later, I casually questioned him about that statement. He informed me since he was now sixteen, his mother regarded him as being too old to receive gifts.

On the last day of school before Christmas, Tom was called to the office to pick up three gifts labeled *To Tom from Santa.* This yuletide summons to the office coincidentally happened all three years that he was in high school. While I was shaking his hand following graduation, he asked me directly if I was Santa. I guess my guilty grin and quick thump on his shoulder gave him the answer he was seeking. He hugged me, thanked me, and walked off toward his future.

Following graduation, he enlisted in the United States Navy and sailed off to boot camp. Later that year the Persian Gulf War erupted, and Tom received his orders: He was being deployed to the war zone. Before leaving on this unsettling mission, he visited me at school in his dress uniform.

Once outside the classroom, he turned toward me with tears in his eyes. In a strained voice, he told me he came to see me because I was the only one who cared about him and frankly admitted that he was scared to death to depart for active military duty. Touched by his words, I held him in my arms and dredged up all the words of encouragement I could muster.

After he left, I went back into my room and released the rest of my tears. I didn't cry because he was going off to war, I cried because the only way he could receive comfort was to be held in the arms of a teacher. Thank God, he came home safely.

John

Recounting John's life reaffirms my belief it was one of the saddest student situations I've ever encountered. If his chaotic childhood were turned into a made-for-TV movie, no one would believe it was not fiction. The first seven uneventful years of his life ended when his mother died of cancer just as he entered second grade.

When John was nine, his father remarried. His new stepmother turned out to be an alcoholic whose abusive treatment of John was despicable. She was a vile woman who did malicious things to John when his father wasn't home. John's father worked second and third shift, so he couldn't be present when his son went to bed.

One night John told his stepmother that he was cold, so she boiled water and dumped it on him. He suffered burns on his hands and face from the scalding hot water. Another night she kept insisting she was going to kill him after he fell asleep. Fearing for his life, John climbed out his bedroom window and cowered in the bushes until his father came home the following morning.

This unspeakable abuse went on for three years, and then John's father died unexpectedly of a heart attack. The stepmother dragged John into the bedroom where the body lay and said to John, "You see your father lying there dead? He's dead because you're such a bad boy!" Now that his father's absence was permanent, John had absolutely no one to stop her.

Subsequently, she chased him around the house with a hatchet. John raced into the bathroom and locked the door. She smashed the door open and viciously hit John on the head with the hatchet, causing a hairline fracture. Ultimately, the alcohol destroyed this woman's mind, and, mercifully for John, she was institutionalized.

John had no choice but to accept an offer to live with his older cousins, and at this juncture in his life he became my student. The Social Security check he received each month provided him with food and clothing. Now abuse of a different sort took place: His cousins used this money to buy themselves a sports car! John's clothes were rags, and the only cooked meals he received were his school lunches. He was always clean, but his clothes were torn and tattered.

A friend of mine with a son about John's size donated a complete wardrobe for this boy to wear. John came to school every day, took clothes out of my closet, and went to the nurse's office to change. At the end of the school day, he reversed the process.

I just couldn't bear watching him suffer any more, so one night I called my wife and four kids together and discussed the feasibility of having John join our family for a while. Since my family already knew about his desperate plight, they all agreed without any hesitation: *Yes, bring him home* was the unanimous consensus.

The next day John was invited to our home for dinner. Following the meal, I told John we wanted him to live with us, and, if he agreed, he would be treated like one of the family. Since he had a job, I informed him he'd have to pay me twelve dollars a week to live in our home. He was more than willing to accept these terms, and we were most willing to accept him.

The day he moved in was one I'll never forget. The baggage from his entire eighteen years of life was crammed into a plywood box. As we watched him unload his "wooden suitcase" in his new bedroom, he patiently explained to us why each item was important to him. I don't think he ever noticed that he was the only one in the room with dry eyes.

Our four kids and John interacted like any other brothers and sisters. There were arguments over whose turn it was to cut the grass or do the dishes, what music to listen to, or any other subject up for debate. Despite the minor squabbles, my family grew to love John, and he loved us in return.

About six weeks after he moved in with us, John unexpectedly poked his head into my classroom one day and – in all sincerity – woefully reported, "Mr. Riffle, Mrs. Riffle has shrunk all my clothes in the dryer!" I asked John how much he weighed, and he automatically informed me his weight was 138 pounds. I urged him to go across the hall to the nurse's suite and have her weigh him. When he returned to my room, I asked him again how much he weighed. Seeming surprised, he revealed that he now tipped the scale at 153 pounds! I laughed and assured him that Mrs. Riffle hadn't shrunk his clothes, but had simply fed him well for the first time in his life.

John's birthday fell on Christmas Day, so Christmas with John was always extra special. We decided to celebrate his birthday a couple of days before December 25th so it didn't get lost in the "Christmas shuffle." On his first birthday with us, while we were cutting his birthday cake, I observed, "Well, John, I guess this is your first cake." As soon as I said it, I knew I had uttered something totally stupid.

Without pretense he answered, "No, I had one when I was seven." I wanted the earth to open up and swallow me whole, and from the looks my family was giving me, that would have been a blessing!

Each year John bought thoughtful Christmas and birthday gifts for each member of the family. He lived with us for more than three years and gradually matured into a fine young man. When he moved out, I returned all of his rent money – I had opened a savings account in his name and had deposited each of his weekly payments.

John is now married with three children and has a home of his own. I hear from him every month or so, and he tells me his kids are driving him crazy. I remind him of our conversations about how abused children tend to repeat the abuse on their own offspring. He assures me he has never once abused them and never will. In spite of John's terrible childhood, he has turned out to be a very stable and level-headed young man

Leigh

Leigh always seemed on the verge of imparting some personal information, yet she never could quite bring herself to divulge what was bothering her. I remember talking to her numerous times and gently asking her if there was something she wanted to share. She had a strange look on her face while always saying no.

One day when all of her unspoken terrors had taken a heavy toll on Leigh, I found her curled into a fetal position in front of my classroom door. Unsightly bloody streaks crisscrossed both her wrists. Fortunately, the nurse's suite was directly across the hall, so I quickly scooped her up and carried her in there. The nurse efficiently disinfected and bandaged her superficial, self-inflicted wrist wounds while I tried to calm her sufficiently to talk to me. In a shaky voice, barely above a whisper, she told me she had been sexually abused by her uncle for the past four years and felt it was her fault. Taking in her forlorn countenance, I realized these wounds penetrated a lot deeper and would be much more difficult to sterilize.

I notified her father immediately; it was 8:30 A.M., and he said he'd be right there. I called the local mental health office, reported this girl needed prompt professional help, and was instructed to bring her right in. Immediate residential treatment was promised. I waited and waited for her father, but he never showed up. I decided it would be detrimental to Leigh to stall any longer, so I took her myself.

Again when we arrived, the staff assured me they had a placement for her. Then the paper work began. When Leigh informed them that her father had no health insurance, the promised placement mysteriously disappeared. I argued the point, but to no avail.

Next, I took her to the local hospital and experienced the same runaround as I had at the mental health office. Hospital personnel informed me they rarely put adolescents in their mental health unit (which is a lie because I've visited some of my students there). I argued the point again, but without achieving any positive results. By this time, Leigh was in a terrible emotional state while I was trying to keep myself under control for her sake.

I decided to take this poor kid back to school and call the head of our local mental health office again. When I got him on the phone, he still insisted there were no placements available. I warned him in no uncertain terms what was going to happen. After reminding him Leigh's actions that day were a call for help that could potentially lead to a more disastrous outcome the next time, I gave him notice that his name and this story would be reported in newspapers and on radio and TV stations in the area. Within ten minutes, she had a placement in a facility near Philadelphia!

Nevertheless, even when I reassured her that she was soon going to be taken care of and that everything would be okay, she was still visibly trembling. Then she made a simple request that touched my heart: "May I take your watch with me?" I must have looked slightly puzzled because she quickly explained, "If I have your watch, I will have you with me."

With all that had transpired that day, I suddenly remembered I hadn't heard from her father. As I guided her down the hallway and out to my car, a disheveled-looking man slowly approached us, staggering sideways with each footstep. I had never known her father was an inveterate alcoholic. Not only had she been sexually abused, she also had to contend with a drunken father!

Leigh was under residential treatment for six or seven weeks, and her attendants told me she would not let *anyone* take my watch. When she returned to school, she seemed to have acquired more poise, self-confidence, and the ability to handle her problem. Leigh is now in her late twenties and appears to be well adjusted. I'm never quite sure that total recovery ever occurs for incest victims because I've seen these people exist for a while without any problems and then suddenly have a relapse. I can only hope that in Leigh's case there will be a more satisfactory outcome.

Peg

I've always believed that, throughout my life, certain children have crossed my path for a reason. My mother, a former English teacher, was the first to ever make that suggestion to me. Over the years I've come in contact with kids who, under normal circumstances, I never would have known. Peg is one of those people.

During the early 1970s, my homeroom always included sophomores with last names beginning with the letters J, K, and L. For some reason, a few years later my letters changed to L, M, and N.

For the first time ever, we were required to keep these same kids in our homeroom for the next three years. In 1974, Peg began her three-year residency in my homeroom.

When I made up my homeroom seating chart, her desk just happened to be next to mine. Also that year she was assigned to two study halls that I proctored. In one, she sat with me at a round table. She was a personable young woman with a beautiful smile that I only rarely glimpsed. I clearly remember my first impression: *For a young girl, she sure looks unhappy most of the time.*

As the first few months of school went by, we began talking about nothing in particular – just school talk. Since I'm a natural-born talker and she was trapped at the table with me, she had no choice but to respond. She was more apt to initiate a conversation in the study where we were the only two at the table. She discussed the normal adolescent subjects while I talked about my three little kids at home and all the mundane happenings that befall a young father.

Eventually, she started sharing more personal matters with me – usually ones involving her friends. I started to pay close attention to her particular circle of acquaintenances at that time. I'm a strong believer that you can often judge kids by the friends they keep, and it didn't take me long to realize that her present companions left something to be desired. On occasion, I made a negative comment about one of her friends, and, like most teenagers, she defended the friend. I never pushed the point, but instead merely switched to another subject. I eventually asked her the question that I have posed to many students over the years: "Do you want to be where your friends are going to be in ten years? If not, you better do something about it right now."

As the year progressed, a bond of trust was forged between us, and Peg felt comfortable broaching any topic for discussion. Occasionally she still said something that led me to believe she knew that what she was doing was not in her best interest. She seemed to be testing the boundaries of her behavior against my approval or disapproval.

When the new school year commenced, we picked up where we had left off. That year the discussions became even more personal, and I started to voice my opinion more emphatically about some of the activities in which she was involved. This unpopular advice didn't make her too happy, and sometimes she refused to talk to me for a week or more. I pretended not to notice her silent treatment. Every morning in homeroom, I greeted her with a "Good morning, Peg," to which she forced a response and then usually ignored me. As the weeks wore on, she resumed talking to me. She didn't like what I had to say, but she was at least willing to listen.

In her senior year, right after Thanksgiving, Peg had a sudden change of heart and admitted that I was right about her friends and that she didn't want to end up like them. I encouraged her to distance herself from them as quickly as possible while also cautioning her that switching friends would be one of the toughest things she has ever done. I warned her of the lonely time looming ahead when she'd have no friends at all because the new friends she sought would avoid her due to the reputation of her old friends. Willing to take the risk, she began the tricky transition right before Christmas.

When school reopened in January, Peg wasn't in homeroom or anywhere else in the building. Extremely concerned, I asked her younger sister what was wrong. As I might have surmised, since she was bereft of friends now, she was too depressed to come to school. I peppered Peg with pep talks on the phone and sent home messages of encouragement with her sister. Three or four weeks passed before she was able to return to school.

Eventually, I noticed that she was developing friendships with a nicer group of kids. In late April, she came running up to me and blurted out that one of the varsity football players had invited her to the prom. At the same time, I approached a friend who was an executive at a local bank about getting Peg a job. He interviewed her, and she was hired as a teller.

Peg, now in her early fortiss with two children and a good job, seems to be a happily adjusted woman. The outcome could not have been better for the girl who had cited as her most vivid senior yearbook memory *"Growing up and changing values."*

Jennifer

One of the most heartwarming moments of my teaching career involved a young woman named Jennifer and a surprise presentation. Jennifer was a regular education student I had tutored throughout the three years she was in high school. As graduation approached, she constantly reminded me to be in the audience that night. I guaranteed her that graduation was one annual event that I always faithfully attended.

Prior to walking down to the stadium for the actual ceremony, the graduating seniors, dressed in their caps and gowns, sit in the auditorium to await last-minute instructions. The faculty assembles in the auditorium lobby and then follows the procession to the stadium. While waiting for all the seniors to arrive, the high school principal asked me to join him at the podium.

Walking down the aisle, I saw Jennifer stand up and approach me with a gift in her hand and tears in her eyes. Tightly gripping the microphone in front of all her peers, she proceeded to share with her audience what I meant to her and that without my help she *never* would have graduated. Shuffling feet and excited murmuring came to a halt as the seniors listened to her words. When she finished speaking, she turned toward me, handed me the gift, and threw her arms around me.

It took incredible courage on her part to bare herself emotionally in front of all her classmates and teachers before making this presentation. The gift was a silver plate embossed with a dove that was encircled by a delicately etched inscription: "A great teacher can make a student's hopes soar." Needless to say, I will never forget Jennifer and how she made my spirits soar that night.

• • • • •

Always encourage your students to do their very best in all their endeavors. Many kids need just a little positive reinforcement to get them motivated. Edward and Mary are prime examples:

Edward

I met Edward (everyone calls him Eddie, but I always make a point of calling him Edward) in the fall of 1997. He was a handsome young man with a quick wit and an engaging personality. On some days he displayed hyperactive behavior, but he was never out of control. He completed his homework and always showed an avid interest in what we were doing in class.

Halfway through his sophomore year, I challenged Edward to make the honor roll by the end of the second term. He automatically figured that goal was unattainable because he had been barely promoted to tenth grade. I passed on to him some good advice given to me many years ago: *Everything is more possible if you believe in yourself.* He agreed to give it his best shot.

Edward's third quarter grades improved, but not quite enough to make the honor roll. Since fourth quarter report cards are mailed home, I was unaware of whether or not he had qualified for this hard-sought ranking. However, it didn't take long for good news to reach me; I received a phone call at home, and he jubilantly announced, "Mr. Riffle, this is *Edward,* and I made the honor roll!"

I couldn't have been happier if it had been one of my own kids. I congratulated him for his diligence and hard work to achieve this honor; then, just before hanging up, I told him that I expected this type of report card every time. He laughed and said, "I'll try, but too many report cards like this and my mom might have a stroke!"

Edward graduated in 2000, and, as he walked by in his cap and gown, I noticed his honor ribbon prominently displayed on his chest. He was also the recipient of our school's Academic Boosters' Significant Academic Improvement Award. I consider Edward a true success and, more importantly, someone to cherish as a friend.

Mary

Mary was a young woman who wanted nothing more to do with school and frequently talked about quitting. I tried to dissuade her from this dead-end decision, but she had her mind made up to drop out of school as soon as possible. The day she signed out of school, I took her aside and told her that the door to my classroom would always be open to her. I added that I hoped she'd reconsider and come back. She adamantly replied, "Never! I'm going out to get a job and make some money."

More than a year later, there was a knock at my door. A downcast and contrite Mary hesitantly stepped through the doorway. Surprised, but happy to see her, I beckoned her further into the room and enquired about her life outside of school. She dropped her head and sheepishly admitted she wanted to return to my class. I placed my hand on her shoulder and simply welcomed her back. I let the *no-good-job-without-a-diploma-speech* die on my lips. That particular discourse clearly wasn't necessary.

Mary returned with genuine enthusiasm and warned the other students about the perils of the *real world*. She didn't graduate until a few months before her twenty-first birthday, but, through perseverance, she reached her goal. Admitting a mistake is very difficult, but Mary did, and I've always respected her for that.

Margaret and Pat

Words of praise and encouragement needn't always be reserved just for students. Attending a recent parents' visitation night were the mother and stepfather of Margaret and Pat. When they were about to leave my room, I asked them if they could wait a moment until the other parents left so that I could talk freely to them about their children. Not knowing whether that was a good or bad request, they looked a bit apprehensive, but agreed to stay a few more minutes.

After closing the door, I turned to them and said, "You should write a book on how to raise super nice kids." Their worried countenances quickly vanished beneath proud smiles. I told them that their children were such a pleasure to teach, and I just wanted them to know that.

They warmly thanked me for sharing these sentiments with them. The mother said it had taken a lot of hard work, and not everything had gone as they had planned. We shook hands, and they left. As far as I was concerned, that was the end of it.

The next day Margaret approached me and told me her mother had gone home the night before and cried over what I had said. She confided that her mother was a recovering drug addict. In fact, her addiction had been so severe years earlier that the state had removed her children from their home. Stunned by this revelation, I could only stare at Margaret as she continued: "Your kind words to my mother made her feel that she was no longer a loser, and that in spite of her past, she had turned her life around and had become a good mother."

I was speechless. Margaret thanked me and returned to her seat. In the minds of her family, my short conversation the night before had brought them full circle. I had just told the parents what I thought about their children, never thinking it would have any more meaning beyond a sincere compliment.

• • • • •

Maintaining two-way communication with students is absolutely necessary. However, some kids are so withdrawn or shy they cannot express themselves verbally. Having these students keep a weekly journal is a less threatening way to interact. Each student is required to write one weekly entry and is encouraged to jot down additional thoughts throughout the week. I've always reserved the first period on Monday for "journal time" because it is usually on the weekend when most "things" happen.

Before anyone begins writing in a journal, I make it perfectly clear that whatever information is shared remains confidential between the two of us. Most times the correspondence will be nothing more than idle chitchat, but I'm always alert for a serious call for help from any one of my students. He or she may not want to confront a serious issue with me directly, but will utilize the written word as a more comfortable form of dialogue.

Donna

Donna repeatedly wrote in her journal about the horrific fights that took place between her mother and father. Often using the appalling language to which she was subjected in that household, she vividly described her awful day-to-day existence at home. Having established a written rapport, she was finally able to request a meeting after school in one of her entries. She also added in a postscript that she wanted to "show" me something.

She quietly slipped into my room at the end of the day and – without saying a word – inserted a cassette into my tape player. To my astonishment and chagrin, she had taped her parents fighting, making me an unwilling eavesdropper. Obviously alcohol was a catalyst in this particular argument. I finally asked her to turn it off as I had heard enough. I turned to talk to her, and she started sobbing. I held her and tried to comfort her.

This circumstance was technically none of my business, yet now – as far as Donna was concerned – it was! These sensitive family situations are difficult to handle and most times are unsolvable, but teachers can always be there to support and guide their students. Donna and I discussed her situation many times because our school at that time didn't have a mental health specialist on staff to help her deal with the problem. Thankfully, schools today offer more services than ever to help students in crisis situations. Nevertheless, I still make abundantly clear to all of my kids that "I'm here for you as long as I live, and all you ever have to do is pick up the telephone and call me day or night." They have taken me at my word.

Jack

"You'll be dead before you're twenty-one," I bluntly warned Jack, a student with a serious drug addiction. He had phoned me at the ungodly hour of 2 A.M. to tell me he had been arrested in a drug sting. Totally amazed that he had been caught, he complained, "Man, the dude had long hair, a leather jacket, and he was riding a Harley." I dryly informed him that's why they call it *undercover police work*! I questioned his decision to call me instead of his parents. "The choice was easy," he replied. "They don't care, but you do." I bailed him out, and he paid me back every penny.

When it came time to exchange yearbook pictures during his senior year, Jack admitted he had not had them taken. The school provides a photographer for those students who haven't had a formal portrait session in the summer. Of course, Jack wasn't dressed well for the occasion, so I took off my sport coat (I doubt if he had ever worn one in his life), shirt, and tie and loaned them to him. He hurriedly donned his "new" outfit and left me standing in my t-shirt. Fortunately, the superintendent or principal didn't choose that particular moment for an unscheduled visit!

Twenty *years* later, he phoned me again, but at a more civilized hour of the day. "Mr. Riffle, this is Jack. Are you still teaching?" After I had affirmed that fact, he said, "Good, because you have a big heart, and kids like me need you." That was one of the most cherished compliments I have ever received.

Warren

I'm reminded of another twenty-year-later phone call, but the purpose behind this belated contact was not to thank me for anything. "Mr. Riffle, my wife wants to have her tubes tied; how do we get that done?" When I could find my voice again, I agreed to help them look into the matter. To say the very least, this wasn't my area of expertise, but I called a clinic at a local hospital and the arrangements were made. Mission accomplished!

Wendy

There are times in my life that my relationships with students create future situations I could never foresee. When I was a young teacher, I taught three sisters who were terrific kids. As adults, two of them moved out of the area, but Wendy, the oldest, married a local man and sent her kids to our school. I taught all four of her children. The standing joke between Wendy and myself was that if I taught long enough, I'd teach her grandchildren, too.

Tragically, the laughter stopped one spring day. Her five-year-old grandson was hit by a car and put on life support in the trauma center of our local hospital. As the family kept a bedside vigil praying for a miraculous recovery, they were told that Justin had no brain function. The heart-wrenching decision to turn off the machine was made, and he slipped away peacefully.

I had been informed about the accident by the child's uncle. Within hours of his death, I received a phone call from the family asking me to attend the funeral. I was stunned by their request, but naturally made arrangements to be there.

Justin's funeral touched me deeply; I had never been in the midst of such sorrow. The image of his daddy's grief-stricken face is etched in my mind forever. My tears flowed with everyone else's as we laid him to rest in that small country cemetery.

Not until months later did I reflect on my involvement with Wendy and her family. They were going through unfathomable heartbreak and still needed to call on me for emotional support. Teaching Wendy, her sisters, and Wendy's children was a great pleasure, but never could I have imagined the impact I had had on their lives.

Glenn

I was involved with junior high school football for many years and met many outstanding kids during my tenure as a coach. In 1979, I had two eighth graders, Glenn and Terry, who were best friends and super nice boys. Following ninth grade, Glenn moved to Texas with his family. On occasion, Terry told me he had talked to Glenn on the phone or had received a letter in the mail. Following their high school graduation, Terry and Glenn both attended college.

One summer day after their sophomore year in college, Terry informed me that Glenn was coming back to see me that weekend. Since I hadn't been in contact with him for over six years, I was curious as to the nature of this visit. I figured it had to do with athletics because football was our common bond.

When the two young men arrived at my house, they expressed a desire to speak to me privately, so we sat at the picnic table in the backyard. I looked at Glenn and knew something was terribly wrong with him, but couldn't imagine what it might be. When I asked him what was troubling him, he started to cry uncontrollably. I just sat there dumbfounded.

While wrapping my arm around Glenn, I glanced over at Terry, seeking some sort of insight into his friend's obviously distraught state of mind. Terry just shook his head, indicating that Glenn had to tell me himself. When Glenn finally got himself under control, he despondently related that his mother and sister had been arrested in a prostitution ring. My mouth must have dropped to my knees; what could I say?

I had not seen this young man in six years, yet he felt compelled to came back to discuss this stressful situation with me, insisting I was the only one who could help him. We sat at that picnic table for hours talking about his problem, and my final advice was really quite simple: I told him that he could not change what his mother or sister had done, that he could control only his own actions.

I admitted my advice was easy for me to give, but certainly not easy for him to follow. However, he agreed with me and said he would do his best to take care of himself. He thanked me, hugged me, and left for Texas the next day. Later I learned that the entire family was under professional care. As when he was on the playing field, Glenn was trying his best to do what I had suggested – but this time he would be calling the rest of the plays.

Rebecca

One afternoon as my students were filing out of my room to go home, I noticed a vaguely familiar woman hovering outside my door in the crowded hallway. When she walked into the brighter illumination of my classroom, I immediately recognized Rebecca, a woman who was now more than twice the age she was when she had last sat in my class.

As I approached her with my arms wide open, she started to sob. Once again I wondered what disastrous life crisis had befallen another former student. Apologetic and fighting back more tears, she reminded me that I had told her to come see me if she ever needed help.

Now in her early forties, Rebecca was married and had two children. Her reason for coming to see me was definitely not a pleasant one: Her husband was beating her. Rebecca chose to confide in me because if she had told her parents, her father would literally have killed her husband!

This was a real dilemma. She wanted to take her two kids and escape this abusive environment, but didn't know where to go. I immediately called a local women's protection agency, which arranged accommodations in protected seclusion for her and the two children.

That solved the immediate major problem, but not the problem of telling her parents. Since I'm acquainted with her mother and dad, I agreed with Rebecca that telling her father could create an explosive situation. Her dad was a nice guy, but woe unto the man who laid a hand on his daughter! We agreed she should talk to her mother privately. This arrangement worked because somehow Rebecca's mother kept her husband from pummeling his soon-to-be ex-son-in-law.

Thankfully, not all phone calls and visits from former students are problematic. Over the years there have been numerous contacts from students who simply want to stay in touch. It's very satisfying and makes my heart smile to know that, after all this time, many of them still consider me a friend they can turn to in good times and in bad.

• • • • •

For educators to wield their influential power over students wisely is an awesome and sometimes downright scary responsibility. For approximately thirty-five hours a week during the school year, young people are in the presence of their teachers. Although powerful competitors such as television, videos, and movies vie for their students' attention, teachers still remain predominant role models in their lives.

Certain kids you will bond with and quickly know that you have made an impact on their lives; what never ceases to amaze me are the ones that went undetected by my teacher radar. We may forget many of our former students, but they will remember us – hopefully for good reasons! Always remember before standing in front of your class: You are a role model for your students, so be an excellent one because you never know where your influence starts and stops.

Mac

My relationship with Mac, who was always an outstanding young man and is now a successful physical therapist, goes back to his days as a high school football player; he was a captain his senior year and an all-conference guard.

One day I stopped him in the hallway to offer congratulations for all of his athletic achievements. After thanking me for my comments, he looked me straight in the eye and said, "Your belief in me motivated me to keep playing."

I must have looked puzzled because he asked, "Don't you remember when I played for you in eighth grade? One night after practice you told me I was a tough kid, and I would be a good football player some day."

I said, "Oh, yeah, I remember that, and I guess I was right." We shook hands, and he walked away.

Truthfully, the only thing I remember about him in football was the first day of practice when he showed up with a violin. I kidded him, "I hope there's a machine gun in that case!"

He answered innocently, "No, coach, there's just a violin in there."

Honestly, I didn't remember the other conversation, but he did, and that's all that matters.

Cortney

During Homecoming Week, our senior class girls traditionally play the underclass girls in a powder puff (flag) football game. As a senior in high school, Courtney decided to participate in this spirited and competitive event.

On the day of the much-heralded match-up, she bounced into my classroom, proudly decked out in her number 81 jersey. Grinning broadly, I assured her 81 was a really "cool" number because those were the same digits on my football shirt in high school.

Rolling her eyes, she exclaimed, "Hello! I know that! Why do you think I'm number 81?"

"How in heaven's name," I asked, "did you know my number?"

"You mentioned it two years ago," she replied matter-of-factly.

Cortney recalled something as trivial as my high school number; it was scary to think what else she remembered! Believe it or not, you talk and they do listen, so be very conscious of what you say.

Kristy

Kristy was a young woman who was in my homeroom in 1979. She and I conversed in the hallway if we saw each other, but never beyond idle conversation. She graduated from high school in 1982, and I never saw her again. However, in 1986, I received a letter from her. An excerpt from this correspondence follows:

"I don't know if you knew it or not, but you made an incredible impact on my life, professional and personal. Professionally, you made teaching a possible career choice - one with rewards, one that makes a difference. Personally, you helped me learn not to take life so seriously."

In 2004, she contacted me again to let me know that she is now a school librarian in Abilene, Texas.

Karen

In 1997, our district superintendent called to ask if I knew a Karen _____. I remembered her, although her brother was more memorable because he had been an outstanding athlete.

The superintendent explained she had just been hired in our district as an elementary special education teacher. As part of the interviewing process, Karen was asked why she wanted to teach in this field. Her answer: "I watched Mr. Riffle with his students, teaching and at the same time caring about them, and I wanted the chance to do that too."

She was a student here twenty-two years ago!

Aunt Betty

A humorous incident happened in 1998 when the niece of a former student was in my class. I'm a major anti-smoking crusader, and one day, while I was pointing out the serious consequences of the smoking habit, this niece tattled, "Well, Mr. Riffle, my Aunt Betty smokes." My eyes widened. "I never thought Betty would smoke," I commented before resuming my lecture.

On Monday, a couple of weeks later, the student told me she had spent some time with her Aunt Betty over the weekend and had mentioned the smoking revelation she had made in class. Her aunt was furious, fuming, "Why did you tell Mr. Riffle that I smoke? What's he going to think of me?"

In spite of myself I had to laugh because Aunt Betty is forty years old, yet she still cared about my opinion of her. It amused me to realize I still had this lingering influence on a former student. Two weeks later Aunt Betty sent me a message: *I'm trying to quit*!

Jeff

In late May of 1997, as I returned to my classroom, a chance meeting that ultimately changed two lives took place. I was greeted by a young man, a special education supervisor, a guidance counselor, a caseworker, and the boy's mother. Jeff and I were introduced to each other; I was told he might attend our school the following year.

Jeff's favorite subject was history. I told him he was in luck because that's one of the courses I teach. Also during our discussion, he disclosed a fanciful wish that he had always kept a secret: the desire to own a medal for bravery. Without hesitation I said, "No problem – because I have a medal for bravery in my closet. Old teachers have everything in their closets!"

I ceremoniously draped the shiny medal, dangling on satiny red-white-and-blue ribbon, around his neck. Impulsively, I picked up a blank piece of paper and recited an improvised commendation for the Congressional Medal of Honor. When I finished my little speech, I smartly saluted him and firmly shook his hand. We both laughed, and I told him he could keep the medal. Jeff stayed a few more minutes and then left with his mother.

I forgot all about the incident until the next day when the special education supervisor came back to my room with tears in her eyes. Concerned, I asked her what was wrong. She said nothing. Finally she smiled and explained, "You have no idea what miracle you performed yesterday, do you?"

Regretting that I couldn't remember such a divine act, I smiled back at her and replied, "What are you talking about?"

She revealed that Jeff suffered from school phobia. In fact, the appointment to visit our school had been made and cancelled four times because each time, as he was about to leave for his visitation, he became physically ill. Apparently, after his visit with me, he told his mother he was willing to attend my class in September on a trial basis. The supervisor fervently thanked me again and left my room. I smiled to myself and thought *I didn't do anything but make Jeff laugh.*

The following September he attended school on a half-day basis, and by November he was managing a full schedule. He excelled in his courses, earned honor-student status, and graduated on schedule with his class.

Jeff changed my life, too. In March of his senior year, he informed me that he had nominated me for the prestigious American Teacher Award that the Walt Disney Corporation presents annually. I thanked him and expressed my appreciation for his kindness.

Jeff mused, "Wouldn't it be great if you won?"

Trying not to dampen his enthusiasm, but wanting him to face reality, I gently replied, "That would be wonderful, but you have to understand that there are teachers so creative they almost work magic in their classrooms."

He looked me straight in the eye and said, "Yes, but you turn lives around."

Startled by his unrehearsed and sincere remark, I glanced at my aide and then back at Jeff. "Jeff, no matter what Disney could ever do, they could not top what you just said!"

Four months later, Disney contacted me, relaying the incredible news that I had won. I couldn't believe my ears; I thought someone was playing a joke on me. The caller confirmed that out of more than

70,000 nominees, I was one of thirty-three honorees for the year 2000. To say the least, I was overwhelmed by this honor.

One of the first people I called was Jeff. Still in a state of disbelief, I informed him that I had won. Without sounding unduly surprised, he smugly replied, "I told you you'd win."

"But Jeff," I protested, "there were more than 70,000 nominees for this award. Do you know what the odds must have been to win this contest?"

Unfazed by my words, he patiently offered his simple rationale: "Mr. Riffle, we all knew you would win; there isn't another teacher anywhere who can match you."

Still feeling undeserving of the award, I sincerely thanked him for his unwavering support.

While in California to accept the award, I retold the story with Jeff's statement about "turning lives around." I always finished the story the same way: "It still stands; what he said has meant more to me than anything Disney can offer."

Kathy

At our local pharmacy recently I mentioned to Kathy, an employee I've known since she was in high school, that I was writing this book.

"Well." she said, "I never would have graduated if you hadn't helped me with my term paper."

I said, "What term paper?"

"I failed my first term paper, and I wasn't going to graduate if I didn't get a passing grade on my second one. How could you forget a term paper on horse racing?"

I admitted that I honestly didn't remember helping her with that paper.

She retorted, "Well, I remember because without your help, I wouldn't have made it!"

Rochelle

Just days before graduation, I stared at Rochelle as she left the room, turned to my aide, and said, "I feel that I've never reached her in the three years I've taught her."

Elaine replied, "You might be surprised; there's more to Rochelle than we know."

I was about to discover the truth behind her observation.

On the very last day of classes, Rochelle came into my room after all the students had left and told me she had something for me. She offered me a handwritten letter and cried as I read it. The letter was emotionally eloquent and one that I will always treasure:

Dear Mr. Riffle,

You probably get millions of these letters, but I think that I should tell you how I feel about you.

I think that you are the most caring person I have ever met. You never judge a person by their looks or their past history. You get to know the person for who they are, not what happened in the past like most teachers. I think every student you have ever had, you made an impact on. I don't know a student that you haven't touched in some way. You are always there for everyone, good or bad, and I respect you for that. I hope one day that I can be as caring and trusting as you are.

You have touched my family in so many ways. My aunts (former students) talk about what a great man you are and my grandparents always thought you were great. My Mom thinks that you are a wonderful man, too. I hope that my sister and all my cousins are as lucky as I was to get to know you.

You made me believe in myself and to not let anyone tell me different. Before I moved into this school district, I thought I would never get anywhere in my life, but you did with your disability, and now I know so can I.

Right now I'm crying because I never realized how much you meant to me! You do mean a lot to me and I will never forget you. You always made me feel good about myself. Before I met you I had low self-esteem, but I don't anymore. I know if I put my mind to it, I can do anything.

I hope this letter means as much to you as it does to me. Thank you for everything you have ever done for me. I never thought that you could love a teacher, but I do love you for believing in me.

Sincerely, Rochelle

Scott

Recently while grocery shopping, I literally bumped into another former student. Scott was a regular education student whom I had befriended during his high school days. We exchanged pleasantries and then, adopting a more serious tone, he said, "I will never forget you coming out onto the football field to hug me after I scored against Pennsbury." I didn't remember that exact incident, but I do recall being with him on the field after every game.

Looking intently at him, I said, "Scott, I want to tell you something that I could never mention to you before. I had noticed early in the season that when the game was over and the other players had their families out on the field, you were left standing there by yourself. I remember telling myself *you will never stand on the field by yourself again.* So after every game, my family and I shed our roles as mere spectators, came out of the stands and down onto the field to be with you."

Scott and I simultaneously welled up with tears. We put our arms around each other right there in the grocery store. He said, "You will never know what that meant to me, and I have never forgotten you."

He reached into his pocket and pulled out a picture of his wife and their two children. He proudly handed it to me saying, "My wife and kids mean everything to me; they are my life. My children will never go through what I went through."

I smiled and said, "They will never stand alone on the field, will they?"

He looked at me through tears and emphatically answered, "No, never!"

I didn't relate the preceding stories to inflate my ego or to pat myself on the back; instead, I specifically choose them to illustrate the far-reaching effect a teacher's words and actions can have on students' lives. An NBA All-Star once said: "I'm a basketball player, not a role model; parents should be their children's role model." That might be his opinion as far as a professional athlete goes, but teachers must realize that they *are* role models – whether they desire that status or not. Just as kids carefully watch and listen to their parents, they also make a habit of scrutinizing the conduct of their teachers. The example set by all educators must be a positive one.

Reading this chapter might give the impression I've *rescued them all.* That certainly hasn't been the case. In fact, I could list the students who didn't respond to advice more quickly than I could name the ones who did. The teacher whose student fails parallels a baseball pitcher who loses a game. That pitcher learns more from losing than he ever does from winning. I have always analyzed each student who didn't succeed in the hope that I could use that knowledge at some later date to help someone else.

Ray

Six weeks before graduation, I had a senior tell me he was quitting school in order to buy a car. I thought he was kidding, but I realized very quickly that he was completely serious. This young man had done very well academically and could have coasted in to graduation. I talked to him at length, but couldn't dissuade him from leaving school.

I saw Ray years later, and he admitted he couldn't get a good job because he didn't have a high school diploma. I have recounted this story dozens of times over the years to steer other "all-knowing" young people away from this avoidable pitfall.

Jim

Back in the early 80s, a painfully shy young man sat very quietly in the back of my class. In his IEP that year I recorded that Jim completed all of his work, put real effort into his studies, but was extremely reserved and would not speak unless spoken to.

One year later when he was totally involved with drugs, my comments changed to *unruly, disrespectful, and very difficult to control.* I never saw a kid undergo a worse transformation in such a short period of time. Helplessly watching a perfectly well-behaved student assume a totally different and irrational personality in one short year was disheartening.

The drug situation in the United States, as in most other countries, is destroying thousands of young lives yearly. It is very difficult, if not impossible, to deal with kids who are "stoned" all of the time. Too often I've seen good kids just go "down the tubes" because of their involvement with drugs.

Sometimes kids will inexplicably fall by the wayside. Just when you think you have an enigmatic child figured out, something profoundly changes in his/her life. The lifelines you toss to these students snap, and there is no bringing them back.

Jacob

I became very fond of one boy I worked with in the late 1990's and had actually considered asking him to live in our home. His own home was in constant chaos, and I thought he could redirect his life in a different environment.

During his sophomore year, his grades improved and his discipline problems decreased. In fact, during the spring semester he helped me produce a videotape on the Kennedy assassination. Three times the following summer, I took him out to lunch just so I could stay in touch with him. My birthday is in June, and he sent me a beautiful card containing a personal message.

Our last get-together was in early August. When school started in September, the boy who showed up in class was not the one with whom I had shared summer lunches. I will never understand what happened during that one-month period. Back in school he became very confrontational; in fact, his behavior worsened to such a degree that he was removed from school and assigned an alternative placement. This young man, in my mind, will always be one of the major, unfathomable failures of my career.

When all the safety nets fail and we lose a student, I always blame myself, thinking I should have been able to devise some infallible plan of prevention. The saddest fact relating to teaching these young people is the realization that you can't reclaim all of them. Therefore, your realistic goal should be to do your own personal best, and *never give up on any kids because you may be all they have.*

CHAPTER 9

"Here!"

... Peter

During my lifetime I have met some very interesting and famous people: Muhammad Ali, astronaut Jim Lovell, and Oprah Winfrey, to name a few. But without a doubt, the people I've admired the most are some of my former students. Admittedly, their names will probably never be nationally known, nor will their special accomplishments be newsworthy enough to capture headlines, but these young people deserve acclamation for the manner in which they have struggled daily with dignity, courage, and grace to rise above their mental and physical limitations.

In the previous chapter the tremendous influence that teachers can unwittingly wield over students was emphasized. Now it is fitting to focus on the opposite and possibly less acknowledged effect: Students can truly have a lasting impact on their teachers' lives. Watching young people succeed under very trying conditions rarely leaves the observer untouched or unchanged. Simply by being in the presence of my students, I have been schooled in lessons of patience, compassion, forgiveness, determination, and perseverance.

Tim

One of the most remarkably motivated young men I have ever met was Tim. Like so many other students I've had over the years, Tim has been a real inspiration to me. We first became acquainted while I was still in college. My cousin Richard was a good friend of Tim's older brother. Tim was an engaging, blond-haired child who faithfully followed me around at my baseball games. I finally bestowed upon him the dubious honor of carrying my equipment back to the car. He was delighted to perform this "prestigious" duty for me.

Unfortunately, I lost track of Tim for a few years because it had become quite evident that he had a learning problem, and his parents sent him to a private school outside of Philadelphia to seek a more favorable educational environment.

Imagine my surprise and pleasure when I again encountered my former "equipment manager" sitting in my ninth-grade class at the beginning of the 1971-72 school year! Tim had enrolled in this particular school district because he wanted to play sports, and our high school is noted for having one of the finest athletic programs in Pennsylvania. He possessed an abundance of athletic ability, and through hard work diligently honed those skills to become a fantastic football player and wrestler. In his junior and senior years he made every all-star team possible and joined the school's elite group of all-time great athletes.

Tim sat in my classes for four years and never stopped amazing me with the things he could do. Despite his severe learning disability, he was very intelligent and had a strong motivation to succeed. He could accomplish anything he put his mind to, even learning to play chess.

Tim started maneuvering chess pieces at a young age. By the time he reached high school there was only one player in the entire school who could beat him, and that boy was the Pennsylvania Novice Champion. The school's Chess Club participants were mostly college preparatory students – and Tim. I attended one of their gatherings and watched an unflappable Tim sitting on a stool surrounded by four chess opponents. He played all four at once and handily won all four games!

Most Sunday nights he matched wits with a local physician. Tim would laugh when recounting endless stories about this doctor "losing his cool" when confronted by a kid who could so easily beat him. I played the "chess king" myself two or three times, and just before my imminent demise, the chessboard would "accidentally" fall to the floor. (Hey, I had to protect my pride, didn't I?) Tim and I still laugh about our notorious chess games.

During his senior year, Tim's parents divorced and went their separate ways. Since he had no place to call home, my family and I extended him an invitation to move in with us until he could find direction in his life. For the next three years this was a real adventure for all of us. Tim became our kids' new uncle, and they loved him.

The summer after high school he enlisted in the U.S. Army because he wanted to be a Ranger. Army Rangers are not just one-dimensional tough guys as portrayed in the movies; they are also highly intelligent people who have to use both their minds and their bodies to survive. Tim assured me he would do whatever was necessary to become a Ranger. His resolve was admirable, but I feared his learning disability would ultimately checkmate his ambitions.

Leaving my reservations unspoken, I watched Tim eagerly depart for Ranger training with his determination to achieve his goal intact. I knew without a doubt that he would be able to handle the physical aspect of training; my concern centered on the bookwork.

In addition to their rigorous routine, Ranger recruits were required to write a lengthy, detailed report every night describing the day's activities. Without exception, all lights in the barracks were out at 10:00 P.M., so everything had to be completed prior to that deadline. Since Tim could never have written his daily report in the allotted time, he laboriously finished it by the dim illumination of a small flashlight. Sitting in a cramped toilet stall with a clipboard and a dictionary, he would stabilize his penlight between clenched teeth and finish his reports sometime after 2:00 A.M. Only then did he go to bed. Reveille brought him to his feet again precisely at 4:30 A.M. He had less than three hours of sleep most nights to gird him for the grueling physical training he had to endure each day.

I can never adequately express how proud we all were when Tim successfully finished training and a few days later marched up our sidewalk arrayed in his Ranger uniform. Like a guided missile unerringly aimed toward a destination, he had reached a goal that everyone thought was beyond his range. With unwavering faith in himself and a burning desire to realize a dream, Tim overcame all physical and mental hurdles that threatened to block his path. The one standard educators have not learned to measure is motivation.

Tim presently lives in Salt Lake City, Utah, with his wife and their three children. He has become a prosperous businessman and owns a beautiful home. I frequently tell Tim's story to my students because, too often, they lack the needed motivation to reach their full potential.

In 1997 Tim and his family flew back East to visit family and friends. He confided that one of the main reasons for the trip was to find an opportunity for him and his wife to talk to me about their one child who is also learning-disabled. I was honored that after all these years Tim still respected me enough to come to me with his problem. I hope that means he has also forgiven all my chess transgressions!

Andy

Andy, a handsome young man I had in class during the mid-seventies, was a pure prototype of a learning-disabled kid. Many students that are classified LD fall into what I call the "gray area". They may be classified as LD, but they have other issues as well. Andy, however, embodied the textbook definition.

He was very intelligent but had a low reading level. He could sit with anyone for hours and discuss whatever subject was broached, and no one would ever guess he had a learning problem. But give him a basic text to read, and it would be shocking to see how much he struggled.

He loved cars and could fix anything mechanical. When he was in my class, he bought his very first car, an old Ford Fairlane station wagon. This vehicle was his pride and joy, and I swear on any given day it would have been possible to eat off the hood. Now, twenty-five years later, he owns a small fleet of show cars. But, believe it or not, he still has that old station wagon. In fact, when I talked to him a while back, I had the audacity to ask him what year he finally sold the old wagon. He looked at me in dismay and said, "Mr. Riffle, I would never sell that car!"

About ten years ago our local paper ran an article on Andy and one of his show cars, which just happened to be a three-time, national-car-show winner. The article described the car and also chronicled how hard Andy had worked to get it in top condition. Even more astonishing was the fact that he had taken the entire car apart and put it back together again without taking any notes. Newspaper readers were probably amazed by this fact. I, of course, knew why he didn't write anything down: Writing was too difficult for him. This reader just felt admiration for a young man who had persevered and did not allow his learning disability to defeat him and force him into a less satisfying occupation.

Douglas

One of the most memorable students I ever encountered was a young man named Douglas. Douglas was small of stature, afflicted with cerebral palsy, but had the heart of a giant. Douglas couldn't walk erectly and had to awkwardly shuffle his feet when moving from place to place, but nothing diverted him from his lifetime goal to become an ordained minister and work with other disabled people.

Unexpectedly on a bitter cold winter morning he asked me if he could switch to another bus. Not knowing what was troubling him, I explained how bus routes were set and generally couldn't be changed this late in the year. He looked terribly upset with my answer. I asked him what was wrong, and after deliberating for a few minutes, he told me.

Three high school students had terrorized him at the bus stop. They stripped his coat down over his arms and held a cigarette lighter to his face. They didn't actually burn him, but they scared him half to death. When they were done bullying him, they hurled him into a snow bank. Because of his palsy, he couldn't free himself from the icy piles of snow. Two junior high students finally helped him to an upright position.

I can't remember ever being madder in my life. Douglas probably weighed only a hundred pounds, while the three kids who intimidated him were big and burly. Those were the days of corporal punishment in school, and, believe me, it was administered! All three kids were suspended from school for two weeks, and were banned from all extracurricular activities.

The one boy's father asked to see me before he removed his son from school. The distraught man told me he was ashamed to call this boy his son and wondered if there was anything he could do. I informed him that Douglas was fearful of future repercussions because he had turned in the boys. The father asked to see Douglas so he could personally assure him that his son would do nothing more to harm him.

I left the principal's office to get Douglas, and by the time we returned, the boy was crying. I'm sure his father had handed out his own punishment in my absence. The boy was slumped in a chair when Douglas walked up behind him, gently put his hand on the boy's shoulder, looked at the father and said, "Don't be too tough on him; he was only trying to have fun." That statement of forgiveness by Douglas cut that boy right to his heart.

I'm sure that kid would much rather have had Douglas punch him in the face than forgive him. Douglas not only believed in his faith, he lived it. When he left school later that year, I found a letter on my desk, one that I have kept for more than thirty years.

Dear Mr. Riffle:

May you always find joy in teaching others with the things Christ has taught you. May all the secrets of knowledge, wisdom, and courage be yours! May the Lord Jesus always educate you, and may you always remain superior in what you teach best, "Love." May the Grace, Peace, Love, and even Jesus Christ himself be with you and your loving blessed family always! Thanks for everything.

Going to make it in the Faith with our Lord and savior Jesus Christ. See you at the church of the future. A servant of our Blessed Lord and savior Jesus Christ, now and forever more.

His, Douglas

John 3:16
For God so loved the world, that he gave his only begotten son, that whosoever believeth in him should not perish, but have everlasting life

Colossians 1:10
That ye might walk worthy of the Lord unto all pleasing, being fruitful in every good work, and increasing in the knowledge of God.

I've known my share of super athletes who were big, strong guys, but I've never known a tougher man of mind or spirit than Douglas. It's been more than thirty years since I've seen him. His memory of me might have faded many years ago, but I will never forget him. I have always felt he made me a better man by the example he set.

Eric

Fortunately, the human spirit is something that can soar above the confines of physical infirmities. Eric was another student affected with cerebral palsy who experienced difficulty with speech and mobility. Nevertheless, the mischievous sparkle in his eyes and accompanying grin endeared him to his teachers and classmates.

Despite his easygoing manner, Eric sported a stubborn streak when told there was something he couldn't do: "What do you mean I can't do that?" would be his offended comeback. Given the opportunities, Eric soon learned to bowl, golf, and drive a manually adapted car, performing all three activities as well as or better than most of us.

He is now thirty years old and the inventory control specialist for three different companies, even being part owner of one of them. *Well, why couldn't he do that!*

Meganne

When she entered tenth grade, Meganne, who had spina bifida, was confined to a wheelchair. We engaged in many private conversations discussing subjects that ran the entire gamut of human emotion. These talks revealed she was angry at her lifelong limitations, but even angrier when she felt others treated her as inferior because of her disabilities.

During her junior year, she was hospitalized for months on end. Gone was our faithful goldfish feeder and the girl who cried "Wah! Wah! Wah" to admonish those who dared to complain about trivial matters. She kept us grounded, and the room was empty without her.

However, I soon realized her spunk had simply relocated to a different building. As weak as she was while lying in her hospital bed, she always managed to tease me when I paid her a visit:

"Are the security guards off duty again?"

"Who left you in?"

"The nurses had specific orders to keep you out!"

But I would discover that Meganne didn't always follow orders either when she had a goal in mind.

The day the picture-taking session for this book was scheduled, Meganne was hospitalized again, this time sixty miles away in Philadelphia. Much to my surprise, before being admitted she had coerced a promise from her parents and the doctor to allow her to come home for Mr. Riffle's photo shoot. They relented and agreed she could have a twelve-hour pass. (If you look at her picture in this book, you will see a hospital ID bracelet on her left wrist.)

Meganne might never take one step out of her wheelchair, but no matter where she goes, she will take great strides as an outspoken proponent for physically challenged children.

Rachel

Rachel, who also had spina bifida, was about 4'2", but her size shouldn't be measured in feet and inches, just in heart and spirit. She acted as if her physical disability was a minor inconvenience. Although she had limited mobility with leg braces and crutches, she spent a great deal of time in a wheelchair. Nevertheless, she played the cello, sang in the school chorus, and participated in basketball and tennis. Moreover, she was also the resident card shark in her family!

One of the first weeks I had her in tenth grade, just to tease her, I let my 6'6" frame tower above her, scowled down at her and said, "Rachel, I'm probably the meanest man you're ever going to know, so don't mess with me!"

Undeterred by my gruff approach, she took my hand and smiled up at me. "Mr. Riffle, you're just a big teddy bear."

My aide looked at me and laughed. "It didn't take her long to figure you out, did it?"

Following graduation, Rachel took a summer course in sign language and entered college that fall majoring in social services. Honestly, because of her positive attitude, I would forget she had a disability. To me she was just Rachel, not *the girl in the wheelchair*. Life did not deal her a very strong hand, but Rachel never folded.

Josh

Josh, a young man virtually immobilized by muscular dystrophy, was another fine student who left a lasting impression. Although he had the use of only two fingers on his right hand, he was able to propel himself around school on his motorized wheelchair and attend regular classes. Even though he was not one of my students, I assisted him with his lunch the three years he was in high school.

What a great kid! Here was a young man almost totally dependent on other people for even the most basic needs, and yet I never heard him complain one time about anything unless, of course, it was about football. He was an ardent sports fan and attended most of our school's football games with his dad. Josh and I shared many sob stories discussing our Philadelphia Eagles.

Having been an avid and informed reader in high school, he went to college and earned a degree in architectural design. We are lucky to have him back working with us at our school in the Technology Education Department.

Fighting Ron

In the history of pugilism there have been many legendary encounters: Louis and Schmeling, Ali and Fraser, Hearns and Leonard, and Mr. Riffle and Ron. Riffle and Ron? Not too many people witnessed this "blood match." Well, actually, this fight never took place.

Fighting Ron, one of my all-time favorite kids, had to deal with macrocephaly and its inherent problems. Although small, he was constantly challenging me to a fistfight. That open invitation lasted for years. Every time he wanted to duke it out, I'd pull a rule from an imaginary book that set forth decisions on the accepted practices for fisticuffs. For example, if he threw down the gauntlet on a Tuesday, I'd inform him that the rulebook said no fighting on any Tuesday that followed a Monday. During every standoff, each combatant glared at the other with a scowl, then backed down reluctantly, promising to take the other to "Knuckle Junction" in the near future.

Even though we reenacted this comedy routine over and over, Ron truly was a fighter. He had a serious health condition that put him in a life-threatening situation three times in four years. Fortunately, each bout he fought back and won. Witnessing Ron's strength and courage has taught me that most of the problems encountered in my daily life are nothing more than temporary setbacks. Ron was a wonderful mentor; he taught me many "life lessons," among them take each day one step at a time.

Peter

One of my students only ever spoke a single word to me. Peter was afflicted with a severe case of cerebral palsy, which rendered him nonverbal and dependent on a wheelchair for the rest of his life. I had known Peter and his loving and supportive parents since he was a young child. During the four years I had him in class, speech eluded him, but he was fluent in the common human language of laughter, which fostered his communication with everyone.

Since one of my history courses covered the Nineteenth Century, I decided a field trip to the Gettysburg Battlefield would provide an excellent educational experience. Under normal circumstances, taking a group of students on a day trip out of the classroom can be a daunting endeavor. Including students with special needs requires extra planning and careful attention to detail. After mentally reviewing the trip several times, I was finally satisfied that I had covered every contingency concerning the motorcoach and the itinerary. The projected trip would be a special day for everyone involved; I just didn't know *how* special.

The excited students began boarding the motorcoach in front of the school at 8 A.M. Peter's father carried his frail son from his wheelchair to his seat on the bus. After shuffling for the umpteenth time through papers I would need for the day's activities, I was satisfied I had everything with me and deemed we were ready to depart. Only a roll call remained.

With an exaggerated flourish, I pulled the list of names out of my shirt pocket. As I stood up in front of the bus and observed all the smiling faces before me, I felt overwhelmingly repaid for all the painstaking preparations. I read off each student's name, carefully listening for individual responses. Without thinking, I called out Peter's name.

I was instantly appalled by my insensitive oversight. My inner voice berated me for this stupid blunder: *How could you plan the perfect trip and then embarrass Peter?* As I was about to make light of the matter, I watched in amazement as Peter's chest seemed to visibly inflate as he rocked backward. With all the willpower he could muster, his head pitched forward and a forcefully expelled "Here!" ricocheted around the bus.

Although the rest of my body froze, my eyes must have widened in disbelief. A moment of almost reverent stillness pervaded the bus, quickly dispelled by the spontaneous cheering of his fellow passengers. With tears stinging my eyes, I completed the roll call and sat down. Now we were ready to travel to *another* battlefield.

The preceding stories are just a sampling of the many I have been privileged to experience while teaching special needs children. Although my job was to intellectually and emotionally nurture these students, the process unexpectedly enriched my own life beyond anything I could have possibly imagined. Every year students come into my life and make an impact on me as a person. They exhibit indomitable spirit and a zest for life that is extraordinary. Do I need to meet more famous people? Hardly. I already stand in the presence of heroes every day that I teach.

CHAPTER **10**

" The clouds are gone; you're now my cloud chaser."
... Mindy

In my attempt to write this book, many problems confronted and confounded me. It was extremely challenging to organize my thoughts and memories, accumulated over a period of thirty-seven years, into a manageable manuscript that would reflect the colorful spectrum of the teaching profession. The final dilemma was the development of an appropriate ending. I ultimately discovered that in writing, as in teaching, I could allow my heart to guide me. As mentioned in the first chapter, this book has been dedicated to Mindy, who appointed me her *cloud chaser*. This is her story.

I had heard about Mindy and her family while she was still in junior high school. She and her two younger siblings were affected by an incurable illness called Batten's Disease. This hereditary disorder, whose early symptoms often don't appear until a child is in elementary school, causes blindness before the teenage years, gradual loss of motor skills, and, eventually, death.

My first meeting with Mindy occurred purely by chance. At a recreational swim one night, I spotted a man with a blind girl. Assuming they were members of this family and desiring to make their acquaintance, I introduced myself to Mindy and her dad Mike. We spoke for only a few minutes, yet Mindy and I bonded instantly. I remember telling her that there weren't too many advantages to being blind, but not seeing me in a bathing suit was certainly one of them!

I knew through the grapevine that her parents and our school district were at odds over certain educational issues described in her IEP (individual educational program). Since I was the only high school learning support teacher certified to teach visually impaired students, I was assigned as her primary teacher.

The spring before Mindy was to enter tenth grade, I attended a transition meeting for her. I walked into the room and immediately sensed the tension. An advocate and a well-known educator of blind students from Philadelphia both accompanied Mindy's family. A lawyer, teachers, and various administrators represented the school district. The lines were drawn for the impending battle.

As anticipated, it soon proved to be a stressful encounter with both sides spewing legal jargon at each other, an ineffectual exchange which did absolutely nothing to benefit Mindy. This verbal volley continued endlessly without anything positive being accomplished. Finally the school district's attorney asked for a recess.

I waited until most people from our district left the room and then approached Mindy's mother, Vicky, to introduce myself. I needed to know directly from the mother what she expected from the school. Without hesitation she looked at me earnestly and simply stated, "I want my daughter to be happy and to feel good about herself."

I nodded and said, "You give her to me, and I promise you that our staff will make that happen."

Vicky challenged, "If it doesn't happen, I'll call you on it."

I said, "No problem, I sincerely want you to." I took a piece of paper and wrote a phone number on it and gave it to her.

She looked at me quizzically and asked, "What's this?"

I replied, "It's my home phone number; when you feel it's time to call me, you will know how to get in touch with me."

Mindy, her family, and I quickly became friends. I found Vicky and Mike to be caring, loving parents who wanted only what was best for their child. We talked frequently about what we could do to help their daughter. By this time I had been told how Mindy's disease would progress. She was so vibrant and full of life that I couldn't believe the prognosis. I felt it had to be a cruel mistake...

On Super Bowl Sunday – January 21, 1979 – our daughter Mindy "touched down" at 4:20 A.M., allowing her dad plenty of time to watch his Dallas Cowboys take on the Pittsburgh Steelers later that day. There were many time-outs called, however, as we took trips to the nursery to gaze in awe at our tiny, sleepy miracle. Our beautiful firstborn child had really arrived and, ready or not, our untested game plan for parenthood would soon be put into play. From that day forward, our lives were never the same.

We were Mindy's most ardent fans as we watched her grow and develop normally during her early childhood years. She was so amazing. Her imagination knew no bounds as her deft, little fingers mastered scissors skills and pummeled Play Doh into colorful creations. It wasn't long before she could roller-skate forward and backward, swim like a fish, and ride like the wind on her bike every day after school in the alley behind our home. Mindy never sidelined herself for long.

The onset of a visual problem manifested itself when Mindy was in first grade. She was soon diagnosed with macular degeneration – a condition that destroys central vision, usually leaving peripheral vision intact. Although the principal of the Catholic school she attended believed that she did not require any special adaptations in school for her problem, he still thought she should receive all the one-on-one help available. It was therefore necessary to dual enroll her, which meant she would still go primarily to Catholic school but would also obtain services from a public school. Yet as parents, we never fully realized how much instruction our child would miss by being pulled from class, and how differently the other children would begin to judge her. Nevertheless, we consented to these plans, trusting the experts to know what was the best way to educate our daughter. So began Mindy's journey down the special education road.

Mindy was able to function for the next few years in her school with a few adaptations. But by fourth grade it was necessary for her to use a cane at night to go into school for her basketball practices. By Christmas of 1988, we noticed a major change in her vision, causing her to constantly walk into things. Then, just six days after giggling girlfriends and ALF (the lovable, furry sit-com character at that time) teamed up to celebrate her tenth birthday at a sleepover party, Mindy was declared legally blind. As Mindy's eyesight faded, so did many of her "friends." It was the last party for which all the kids showed up for the blind girl.

Our lives changed drastically. I was attending so many meetings now for my daughter. Still in shock about Mindy's diagnosis, I had to deal with an ever-increasing staff of teachers and endless paperwork. I was simply overwhelmed and would break down crying in front of these strangers. I didn't want to believe it was my daughter they were calling blind. I waited and prayed for a miraculous recovery that never happened. I guess we had already been allotted our one miracle – Mindy.

Our first disagreeable encounter with the special education system occurred when we were informed that Mindy was not going to be accessed by the intermediate unit while attending Catholic school. During that meeting, believe it or not, I was told I was an uncaring parent! This triggered a fight to procure the best education possible for my blind daughter without sending her away from her home school, a goal also sought by the school itself. Educational lawyers stated that our case could have set a precedent in the Catholic school system, but the diocese of our church would agree and then disagree. The exact words were: "Mrs. ____, we were reluctant to get back to you about your case because we feel it will jeopardize another case already pending in that district." So Mindy was placed in the public school system, one that was promising us more help for our daughter.

In seventh grade Mindy packed away her school uniforms and made her bold entrance into the public junior high school. The problem still confronting us was how to best educate a blind child – our blind child. We were now more reserved and doubtful about trusting the system. For the next three years, I became more closely involved in the decisions being made concerning Mindy's education. I wanted to discontinue the use of audiotapes because they simply didn't work. I also requested that Braille textbooks be ordered in spring so that they would be available for Mindy to use in the fall. Many hours were spent on the phone talking to whoever would listen. The words "Mindy's mom" soon made the staff cringe. Rather than admit that the school had no viable program for the blind and was fumbling to establish one, the school inferred that we were expecting too much. We viewed it as only wanting what was best for our daughter.

Before entering tenth grade, Mindy's physical condition began to deteriorate even further. The diagnosis was in and it wasn't a good one – our daughter had Batten's Disease. Educational decisions became even more crucial, and we felt the goals in her IEP were woefully inadequate. Disagreements with the school district and some of the teaching staff intensified prior to Mindy starting high school. A pivotal meeting was scheduled to review her IEP and to reach a reasonable compromise.

On the day of the meeting, my husband and I arrived with our own staff. Supporting us was a woman who had her Ph.D. in educating the blind and had written several papers on the subject, a man who was a special needs advocate, and another woman who was a mental health advocate. A lawyer, the head of special education, and a small staff of teachers and administrators were there to back the school district. Tension was high between the two groups; the school district was worried about our intentions, and we were worried about our daughter.

About fifteen minutes into this heated discussion concerning our daughter's future educational goals, a teacher with whom we were not familiar spoke out. His name was Peter Riffle. After listening to his candid comments and the promises he made to us, our faith in the system was partially restored. I remember leaving that meeting fearing that this man's remarks would cost him his teaching job in the school district. That was the day my family met our daughter Mindy's cloud chaser, someone who had actually heard her parents' cry. And so began our pure enjoyment harassing one of the biggest Eagles fans we know. It is Peter Riffle who continues to chase clouds for our family. We love you, Pete. Thanks.

Mindy's mother

…Every day I met Mindy and her mom or dad at the curb and walked with her as she caned her way to my classroom. One day when Mike dropped Mindy off, I noticed a Dallas Cowboys license plate on the front of his van. I was appalled. I said, "Mike, the Cowboys! You're kidding, right?"

Mike said, "No way! Go 'Boys!" Thus began our ongoing rivalry between my Eagles and their Cowboys. Throughout the football season Mindy and her parents would "bust" on me about rooting for the lowly Eagles.

During her years with me, the Eagles rarely beat the Cowboys, but when they did, I exulted. I would Braille something like "Go Eagles Go" and stick it on Mindy's desk. Most Sunday evenings Mike and I talked to each other about the day's games. We didn't realize it then, but we were developing a lasting friendship.

When Halloween arrived that October, Mindy had a festive party for all of her friends. There were three very popular girls in my class I had nicknamed "The Three Amigos." Mindy invited these girls to her party. I was concerned that they would think the affair was too unsophisticated and not show up, but while I was at the home that night talking to Mike, "The Three Amigos" walked in. They danced and mingled with everyone who was there. I was so proud of those girls and commended them for giving up a Friday night with their own friends to attend Mindy's party. They seemed surprised by my sentiments and assured me they had come because Mindy *was* their friend

When Mindy was in tenth grade, I didn't see her as being different from any of my other students. The first signs of her disease became apparent to me during the spring of her junior year. She was beginning to lose her balance and at times becoming forgetful. I always walked next to her as a precaution against her falling. Sadly, I realized she was starting to deteriorate before my eyes.

Mindy was eventually placed in a wheelchair to be taken from class to class. As time went by, she was in the chair permanently. Her incurable disease now noticeably affected her intellect and dulled her senses, but her sweet personality and infectious giggle gave us hope and kept the dire prognosis at bay.

She had the special ability to lift up the spirits of the people around her. I constantly teased her about the Cowboys, particularly picking on Troy Aikman, their all-star quarterback. Anytime I noticed her frowning or upset, I could brighten her mood by simply mocking her team. I remember her bringing sympathy gifts to school when the 'Boys beat my Birds. I invariably threatened her with summer school for the rest of her life. She didn't seem too terrified, sitting there and laughing at me.

By her third year in the high school, the disease had advanced to another level. She was no longer able to function in the learning support classes as she once had. It was decided that she would participate in our school's graduation ceremony that June. It was a happy day for Mindy, but a heartbreaking day for me; what I had feared was obviously now a reality. Nevertheless, in spite of everything she was going through, her friendliness to others never wavered.

Mindy returned to school for two more years for social reasons. School was a place where she had friends and felt at home. Her cognitive abilities were greatly diminished, but she still excelled at bringing joy into the lives of those around her, a precious skill that always garnered her high honors.

Mindy's condition began to worsen on May 13, 2000. I was called to the phone at 1 o'clock that Saturday afternoon. It was Mike. He said, "Pete, you're always there for our kids, and now I need you." The anguish in his voice was unmistakable; then he began to weep. I promised him I would be right there.

I rushed over to their house, and when Mike opened the door, he put his arms around me and despairingly confessed, "I'm not ready for this yet." He told me that Mindy had suffered a seizure with coma-like symptoms during the night and had been taken to the hospital. Mike and I talked for two or three hours, one father to another. I did my best to try and comfort him, but the fear of soon losing Mindy gnawed at my heart as well.

When I arrived at the hospital, I quietly entered Mindy's room and saw Vicky sitting next to her daughter, lovingly stroking her arm. We held each other in a consoling embrace before I sat down.

While keeping our vigil, Vicky looked at me and said, "Mindy would be so happy to know her cloud chaser was here." When I heard that, I broke down and cried because I never felt more powerless in my life.

I looked helplessly at Vicky and said, "But I can't chase these clouds."

She soothingly replied, "I know that; it's just important that you're here." I went home that night and prayed to God to give the parents the strength to endure this unbearable situation.

The next day was Mother's Day. At 4:30 that afternoon, I called the hospital to see if there was any change in Mindy's condition. A nurse who was sitting with Mindy answered the phone and reported that she was stable, but still unresponsive. I told her who I was and that I was a friend of the family. She informed me that the parents had told her about my relationship with their daughter. Impulsively she asked me if I could come into the hospital because my presence might help stimulate some kind of reaction. I said I'd be right there. I kissed my mother and told her I was sorry to leave so abruptly, but I had to go to the hospital and give it my best shot. I wasn't ready to let go of Mindy either.

When I arrived at her room, the nurse who had answered the phone was still on duty. We talked briefly and then she left the room. I sat next to Mindy, held her hand, and quietly spoke to her. For some unknown reason I started teasing her about Troy Aikman, and she began to laugh. I couldn't believe what was happening: This young woman was not acknowledging anything else, yet was responding to my silly story about a football player. The nurses were amazed and told me to keep talking.

Mindy didn't react to anything else I said, but as soon as I teased her about Troy, she would start to giggle again. I was still talking to her about an hour later when her eyes suddenly opened! I bolted right out of my chair and went running to the nurse's station. We all rushed down the hall to the room and, sure enough, she was awake.

Mindy gently squeezed my hand but refused to let me kiss her cheek. Our Mindy was back; she was alert, yet very tired. She remained aware of her surroundings for about an hour and then went back to sleep. The nurse jokingly ordered me not to leave the hospital because she was going to bottle me and keep me for future use. I told her I had no idea why Mindy reacted to my teasing. The nurse made a quick diagnosis: "It's very obvious that you and Mindy share a very deep bond."

When I checked on Mindy the next day, she was sitting up and smiling. And, I did get a kiss and a hug that day! Vicky told me she was doing better, but now refused to eat. As I sat talking with Mindy, I decided to try and feed her…and she started eating! She ate an entire jar of applesauce and drank some water. When Vicky came back to the room, she laughed and accusingly said, "Riffle, are you eating my kid's food again?"

Visits to Mindy became part of my daily routine. Her condition was deteriorating, and there was nothing that could be done to stop her decline. This insidious phase of her illness caused us all unbelievable stress. Since she was responding to me, I unwisely allowed myself to believe that maybe I could somehow save her. I thought that if I could keep her awake and encourage her to interact, she might miraculously recover. Rationally I knew this couldn't happen, but emotionally I couldn't face her impending death.

She was eating less and less food as time went on. I visited Mindy on my birthday in June, and Vicky brought ice cream to celebrate. I fed Mindy a little of the frozen treat and, to my knowledge, that was the last food she ate. Vicky and Mike were resigned to their daughter's fate and somehow found the strength to sustain them throughout their nightmarish ordeal.

Shortly thereafter Mindy was sent home because the hospital could do no more for her. Thus began a two-month vigil by Mindy's family and friends as she lay in a coma-like state most of the time. The strange fact remained that when I visited her, she responded to my voice with a smile and kissed my cheek.

On September 4, 2000, I received an urgent phone call from Mike. He whispered, "Pete, Mindy's going home to God." I ran to my car and rushed to Mindy's house. As soon as I stepped inside the door, she took her last breath and was gone. I stood at her bedside with Mike and Vicky looking at her lying there so peaceful with her cat curled up next to her. A paralyzing numbness overtook me. I collapsed on the floor, my mind blank, but I do remember Vicky holding me in her arms trying to comfort me.

As we sat with Mindy awaiting the funeral director, Mike turned to me and sadly observed, "Pete, we have to go through this two more times." What could I have said to console this father who had just lost his oldest child moments before and knows his other two children are also terminally ill? I didn't speak; I just walked over and clamped my arms around him in a tight hug.

When the funeral director arrived, we all gathered in the next room (including the cat) and shut the door. I will never forget that cat. As they were preparing to take her body out of the house, the frantic animal, trying in vain to be at Mindy's side once more, incessantly pawed the door. Two weeks after she died her beloved pet disappeared, never to return.

Driving the two short miles back to my home seemed an interminable journey; I could barely keep my attention focused on the road. My mind, restless as Mindy's cat, searched in vain for a reason to explain her death. I couldn't shake the mental images of Mindy's last moments. I wanted her back again. I felt like a part of me had died with her; in fact, she did take a piece of my heart with her that day.

Mindy's funeral was held on a bright, cloudless September day. It was a memorable celebration of her gentle life and the people she had touched on her short journey. The only feeling to rival the collective sadness in the church was the bittersweet admiration we all felt for the grieving parents. With remarkable dignity and composure, Vicky comforted Mindy's younger sister and brother while Mike delivered a poignant eulogy that included affectionate tributes to his wife, their two children, and their friends. His uplifting recollections mingled with our own silently cherished remembrances. The daughter he so lovingly memorialized will live on in our hearts forever.

I may have chased your clouds away, Mindy – but you showed me the rainbow.

This book was written to help prepare you for your first few years of teaching. If there is only one thought that you glean from the information and anecdotes found within these pages let it be…

"TEACH WITH YOUR HEART."